Jiddu Krishnamurti

Jiddu Krishnamurti

Life of a Teacher Who Refused Authority

SHUVENDU PATNAIK

First edition, 2026

ISBN: 978-93-5812-129-2

Published by
Shuvendu Patnaik

Gurgaon, India

The information in this book is for educational and informational purposes only. While every effort has been made to ensure accuracy, the author assumes no responsibility for errors or omissions. The views and interpretations expressed in this biography are those of the author and do not necessarily reflect the official positions of any foundations or organisations associated with the subject.

Cover photograph of Jiddu Krishnamurti courtesy of the Krishnamurti Foundation Trust (kfoundation.org). Photographer unknown. Use of this photograph does not imply endorsement by the Foundation.

Contents

Who Was Krishnamurti?

Across the world, people still speak of him, long after his voice has fallen silent.

Some called him one of the greatest spiritual teachers of the modern age. Yet he refused every such title.

He did not want followers. He did not found a religion. He did not gather disciples around him.

Instead, he asked something simple, yet demanding. Can you look at your own life directly, without fear, without belief, without depending on anyone else?

To understand him is not easy. His life did not move in a straight line. The story you are about to read does not follow time step by step. It moves as life itself moves, touching moments that reveal the man, the questions he asked, and the way he saw the world.

Krishnamurti was born in India. Yet he did not belong to India alone. He spoke to people everywhere, not as Indians or Europeans or Americans, but simply as human beings.

What made him different was not where he was born, but what he refused.

He refused authority in matters of the spirit. He refused to stand above others. He refused to become someone to be followed.

One sentence of his became known around the world.

'Truth is a pathless land.'

What did he mean by this?

The writer Henry Miller once tried to describe him.

'If he had a mission, it is to strip men of their illusions and delusions... and thus give back to humanity its full majesty and strength. If any man living merits the title 'World Teacher,' he does.'

To understand this, we must turn to his life—go back to the beginning.

This book is not just the story of his life. It invites a deeper inquiry.

As his life unfolds, certain questions begin to take shape quietly on their own.

Birth of Krishnamurti

It was the night of 11 May 1895. The small town of Madanapalle in South India lay quiet under the open sky. Gentle hills surrounded it. The streets were still. Most houses were dark.

A soft glow lingered in the sky. The full moon had just passed. Around this time each year, Buddhists celebrate Vesak, the full moon that marks the birth and enlightenment of the Buddha. In India, this full moon is also known as Buddha Purnima and is considered especially sacred. That night marked the beginning of the waning moon.

Sanjeevamma sat in the puja room of her modest two-storey house, before a picture of her beloved deity, Sri Krishna, praying softly. She was a deeply religious woman and was expecting her eighth child. She wished that when the baby was born, the name of her God would be on her lips.

As she sat there, the image of Sri Krishna seemed to come alive before her eyes. Within it she saw many smaller images, one within another, stretching inward. A quiet certainty filled her heart. She felt that this child would be special in some way.

A cousin with experience as a midwife had already been called to help. Soon, labour began. Just after midnight, at half past twelve, a baby boy was born. Unlike her earlier deliveries, this one was quick and easy.

Outside the room stood her husband, Narayaniah, holding a watch. He believed strongly in astrology, and the exact moment of birth mattered to him.

The next day, he visited a well-known astrologer, Kumara Shrowtulu, who prepared the child's horoscope. After studying the horoscope, the astrologer looked up and said that this boy would one day grow into a great and remarkable man.

According to family custom, the baby was named on the sixth day. He was called Krishnamurti. 'Krishna' was the name of Sanjeevamma's beloved deity, who himself had been an eighth child. 'Murti' means form or embodiment. At home, they simply called him Krishna.

The family name was first written in English as Geddu Krishnamurti. Geddu came from a small coastal village where the family had lived for generations. Over time, the spelling was changed legally to Jiddu Krishnamurti so that it would be pronounced correctly.

Krishna was born into a respected Telugu Brahmin family. His father, Narayaniah, was educated and held an important position in the Revenue Department of the British Government in the Madras Presidency. In those days, the Madras Presidency covered much of South India, including present-day Andhra Pradesh, Tamil Nadu, Karnataka, Kerala, and parts of Telangana and Odisha.

Through hard work and integrity, Narayaniah rose to become a chief administrative and revenue officer. He was known for his honesty, courage, and generosity.

Krishna's grandfather and great-grandfather had also been learned men, scholars of Sanskrit and respected officials. Education, discipline, and religious observance were strong traditions in the family.

His mother, Sanjeevamma, was a gentle and deeply spiritual woman. She had a melodious voice and often sang devotional songs at home. She was generous, intuitive, and sensitive to the feelings of others.

People believed she had a rare gift known as clairvoyance. This word means 'clear seeing'. It refers to the ability to sense things beyond ordinary sight. She was said to see a soft glow, or aura, around people. Such beliefs were part of the spiritual world in which the family lived.

Sanjeevamma had eleven children in all. Three were born after Krishna. Of the eleven, only six survived beyond childhood, two girls and four boys, including Krishna.

The family followed strict religious customs. They were pure vegetarians. In those days, caste rules were observed very strictly. Visitors from outside the caste were not allowed in the kitchen. Even the shadow of a European falling on cooked food was believed to make it impure. After European visitors left, rooms were washed carefully. Such were the social customs of that time.

This was the world into which Krishna was born. It was a world of faith, tradition, discipline, and deep belief.

The Quiet Years

Krishna grew up as a weak and unwell child. He suffered from frequent fevers and nosebleeds. Because of his poor health, he spent much of his time indoors, close to his affectionate mother. He showed little interest in games, and even less in learning. He seemed content simply to sit and watch.

Narayaniah held a transferable government post. About eighteen months after Krishna's birth, he was transferred to Cuddapah, a much larger district headquarters town to the east of Madanapalle. Cuddapah was known for malaria. When Krishna was barely two years old, he was struck down severely by the disease. For a time, the family almost lost hope of seeing him survive.

In 1898, when Krishna was three years old, Sanjeevamma gave birth to her ninth child, Nityananda. They called him Nitya at home. Krishna soon grew deeply fond of his younger brother.

Unlike Krishna, Nitya was bright and lively. He loved his elder brother dearly and became devoted to him. The two were so inseparable that they were often compared to the Ram–Lakshman brothers of Hindu mythology.

Narayaniah's eldest son, Sivaram, was much older than both of them. He had his own circle of friends and was not especially close to either Krishna or Nitya.

By 1900, Narayaniah's transfers had brought the family to Kadiri, a town larger than Madanapalle, though smaller than Cuddapah. It lay about forty-five miles to the west of Madanapalle.

At Kadiri, when Krishna was six years old, he underwent the sacred thread ceremony. This ceremony was essential for Brahmin families and marked a boy's formal entry into religious life and learning.

Sacred vows were taken through elaborate rituals. A multi-stranded sacred thread was placed across his left shoulder, resting diagonally at the waist. This thread, worn for life by all Brahmins, is treated with deep reverence and is not removed thereafter.

Krishna went through the ceremony quietly and obediently. Seated on his father's lap, he watched closely as the rituals unfolded. Narayaniah held a silver plate filled with rice grains. Sanjeevamma gently guided Krishna's index finger to trace the sacred sound Aum on the rice. The priest chanted mantras as the letter took shape beneath the child's finger.

When the ceremony ended, Krishna was taken to the great Sri Lakshmi Narasimhaswami Temple, which stood atop a lonely hill. From there, Narayaniah drove him to a nearby school.

At the school, a teacher held the boy's finger and guided him once more to trace the letter Aum, this time on sand. This marked the traditional beginning of learning for Krishna.

Krishna was now a Brahmachari, a student expected to live with discipline, simplicity, and restraint. He had been formally set upon the path of learning.

Soon after, Krishna joined a school at Kadiri. Each day, he walked to school with his elder brother, Sivaram. Three-year-old Nitya was deeply attached to Krishna and would not leave his side at home. He always longed to go to school with him.

Late in the afternoon, Sanjeevamma waited for her sons to return from school. She would then walk with them to the Sri Lakshmi Narasimhaswami Temple for the evening prayers. The temple lay about two miles away, and the climb over the stony ground was difficult.

Krishna loved to walk beside his mother along the long, stony path to the temple. Nitya, too, loved to come along, trotting beside them on his tiny legs.

Krishna's ill health often kept him away from school. He also struggled with his studies and showed little liking for learning from books. School held no real interest for him.

Instead, he preferred to spend long hours with his mother in the puja room.

There, Sanjeevamma spoke to him about karma, reincarnation, and other ideas from Hindu philosophy. She read aloud from the great epics, the Mahabharata and the Ramayana, stories he always loved to hear. Yet, as he later wrote in his unpublished childhood memoirs, he could never truly understand them.

Images and idols of gods are considered sacred in Hindu homes and are worshipped daily in a puja room. It was unusual that Sanjeevamma, an orthodox Hindu woman, had a sari-clad portrait of Annie Besant, an Englishwoman, among her household gods.

She often spoke about this lady's greatness with reverence and affection while explaining karma, reincarnation, and other spiritual ideas to Krishna.

Annie Besant was then the President of the Theosophical Society, a spiritual organisation founded in the West. Narayaniah, too, held this English lady in high regard.

Though an orthodox Hindu, Narayaniah had become actively involved in the Theosophical movement and was deeply committed to the Society's work and ideals.

In 1902, Sanjeevamma gave birth to her tenth child, Sadananda. He was the only child in the family born with a mental disability. Though slow in development, he grew into a cheerful and playful boy, deeply loved by everyone at home.

Sanjeevamma later gave birth to an eleventh child, who died in infancy.

The Dreamy Boy

Krishna grew up as a quiet and withdrawn child. He often stood for long stretches of time, gazing at the sky with his mouth slightly open, watching clouds drift slowly across it or trees sway in the wind.

At other times, he would sit on the ground, absorbed in watching ants or other tiny insects. If something caught his attention, he would look at it patiently for hours.

His distant expression, his constant look of wonder, and his habit of staring without speaking made people think he was slow. He also struggled greatly at school.

Krishna's poor health often kept him away from school. Once he missed an entire year of classes. His father's frequent transfers made matters worse, and he soon fell far behind other boys of his age. Many considered him dull. He disliked book learning and showed little interest in lessons.

People often compared him with his youngest brother, Sadananda, who had been born with a mental disability. Krishna was not disabled, but his blankness made others assume he was. No one, not even his father, could imagine how such a boy might one day grow into someone 'wonderful and great'. Yet one man remained certain.

The astrologer Kumar Shrowtulu never wavered in his belief. Whenever he met Narayaniah, he asked about

Krishna. Each time, he assured the father that his prediction could not be wrong.

Many decades later, another Indian astrologer, T. S. Kelkar, re-cast Krishnamurti's horoscope and arrived at different planetary positions. Yet he reached a similar conclusion.

Kelkar described him as a Rajarshi, one in whom deep knowledge arises from within, without the study of scriptures or spiritual discipline.

Such words seemed impossible to come true. Learning never came easily to him. His mind appeared strangely empty.

Looking back many decades later, Krishnamurti himself said that as a boy he had a 'vacant mind', a mind that observed everything yet absorbed nothing.

There was another side to Krishna that showed itself as clearly as his dullness. It was his natural generosity.

When he attended school at Kadiri, he would give away his pencil, slate, or book to any poor boy who needed it. When beggars came to the house in the morning, he would pour all the rice grains into the first beggar's bowl and then run back to the kitchen for more. In the evenings, when beggars came again, he would rush to fetch food for them, even as the servants tried to drive them away.

Krishna loved the sweet dishes and delicacies his mother prepared. Yet he would give away most of his share to his brothers. Nitya often asked for more, and Krishna never refused him anything.

One striking quality of the boy was his complete absence of self-importance. By this time, his father had become a District Magistrate, a position of great authority, and the family had several servants. Yet during picnics with his elder brother and friends, Krishna insisted on carrying all the food himself. He would not allow the servants to do even the simplest tasks for his personal comfort.

It was also surprising that, despite his struggles in school, Krishna showed a strong fascination for mechanical objects. He could take apart complicated gadgets and patiently put them back together. Once, he dismantled his father's watch and refused to go to school, or even eat, until he had reassembled it.

Those who considered him slow or incapable rarely noticed this side.

His close observation of nature, his generous spirit, his lack of self-importance, and his keen interest in mechanical things remained with him throughout his later life.

He also seemed unusually sensitive to things others could not sense. As a child, he said he could see fairies. One of them, he said, was especially talkative and became his childhood playmate.

Some may wonder whether fairies are real. Just as we share the world with birds, animals, and insects, there may also be other kinds of beings that move quietly and remain hidden from ordinary sight. Fairies are believed to be among them.

The young Krishna said he could see and even communicate with fairies. For him, it was simply part of his world as a child, a world close to nature, quiet and free from fear.

Narayaniah did not remain in Kadiri for long. In 1903, after several transfers, he was posted again to Cuddapah. There, a year later, the family suffered a great loss. Krishna's eldest sister died at the age of twenty. She was an affectionate and spiritually inclined young woman. Her sudden death filled the household with grief.

It was during this time that something unusual was noticed in Krishna. He said he could see his dead sister. Narayaniah already knew that his wife, Sanjeevamma, was clairvoyant. Now Krishna seemed to have this ability too.

There was a place in the garden where Sanjeevamma would visit and see her dead daughter. Sometimes she took Krishna along. At first he laughed. Then he said he could see her too. From then on, he said he could always see his dead sister.

The experience frightened him deeply at first. He had seen her body on the funeral pyre, and the memory filled him with fear. He would run to his mother and cling to her. Sanjeevamma held him close and told him there was nothing to fear.

Death, for the little boy, did not feel like something far away. It felt close and real. Perhaps that is why he later seemed to notice things that other children did not even think about.

Krishna was the only one, besides his mother, who spoke of such visions. Others believed him but could never see the dead.

Krishnamurti later wrote about these experiences himself. He said that his mother could sometimes see auras, and he could see them too.

Sanjeevamma believed her son was neither dull nor ordinary. A devoted mother, she cared deeply for all her children. Yet Krishna remained especially close to her. He was her special child.

The deepest blow came in 1905, when Sanjeevamma died. Krishna was barely ten years old. With her passing, he lost the warmth and care that had meant more to him than anything else.

After her death, he often felt her presence. At times, as he walked to school, he heard the soft sound of her bangles, as if she were following him. During rituals, he said he could see her partake of the food offered in the after-death ceremonies.

These experiences were not dismissed. Narayaniah himself later noted the boy's unusual sensitivity.

After his wife's death, Narayaniah took leave and moved the family to Madanapalle. The boys joined school. Without their mother's care, the younger children were often left to themselves.

Krishna grew weak and frequently ill. These became the loneliest years of his childhood.

So passed the early years of his life, quiet, sorrowful, and largely unnoticed.

No one around him could have imagined how soon his life would change.

The Theosophical Society

Krishna's childhood was unfolding amid grief. He had lost a caring and devoted mother, and his busy father could give him little time.

Far away, something else was taking shape. A spiritual movement known as the Theosophical Society had come into being in America. It had begun nearly two decades earlier and was slowly spreading across the world.

Theosophy is often described as a wisdom-religion. It seeks to understand matter, life, and consciousness, and asks some of the largest questions of all. Where did we come from? Why are we here? Where are we going?

Some see it as a way of living rightly. Others see it as a set of universal laws believed to guide the universe. It has also been described as philosophy, religion, and science combined, pointing toward a deeper truth beneath all three.

It speaks of the hidden side of nature, of realities that cannot normally be seen but may sometimes be sensed or experienced. To explain these deeper truths, it draws upon ideas and words from many traditions. Similar ideas can be found in the philosophies of India, China, Egypt, Greece, Palestine, and Arabia, though often expressed in different ways.

Over time, these ideas were written down and shared widely through books, bringing together teachings drawn from ancient traditions as well as reflections on newer discoveries in science.

One of its important teachings is that human beings are not the highest level of consciousness in the universe. Beyond the human stage, it speaks of higher levels of awareness. Adepts, or Masters, are believed to be beings who have advanced far beyond the ordinary stage. They stand at a higher level of development.

These Masters are regarded as enlightened teachers who guide the progress of humanity quietly without seeking recognition. Because their understanding is said to be much deeper than that of most people, they are not easily recognised in ordinary life.

They are described as existing in subtler forms of awareness rather than in physical bodies like ours. For that reason, they cannot be seen with ordinary physical sight. Yet they are believed to possess deep insight into the hidden workings of nature and to guide those who have reached a more advanced stage of understanding.

Much of the knowledge taught in Theosophy is said to have come from such Masters. They are believed to communicate with spiritually advanced individuals through thought-transfer and other subtle means.

Just as human beings belong to the human kingdom of life, these Adepts are said to belong to a higher order of evolution known as the Dhyan-Chohanic Kingdom of Life.

The teachings also speak of communities of such Adepts. The most well-known of these is called the Great White Brotherhood, believed to preserve ancient occult wisdom and guard the deeper knowledge of the Earth.

The Theosophical Society itself was said to have been formed under the guidance of certain Masters of this Brotherhood, notably Master Morya and Master Koot Hoomi.

Helena Petrovna Blavatsky (1831–1891), popularly known as Madame Blavatsky, or simply HPB, was born into Russian nobility. She was a woman of remarkable psychic insight and became one of the central figures of this movement.

It is said that the Masters guided her to seek out Colonel Henry Steele Olcott and William Quan Judge in 1873. Two years later, in 1875, she founded the Theosophical Society in New York with Colonel Olcott, Judge, and fourteen other like-minded seekers. After the Society was formed, Colonel Olcott became its founder-President.

The Society welcomed people of all religions. One of its central principles was universal brotherhood, the idea that all human beings belong to one family.

Yet many who were part of this movement believed it also had a deeper purpose.

Before her death in 1891, Madame Blavatsky indicated that the Society existed not only to share ideas. It also aimed to prepare the world for the coming of a great spiritual teacher, one who would guide humanity into a new stage of understanding.

In different traditions, such a being was known by different names. Some called such a teacher an Avatar, others a Messiah, and still others a World Teacher.

As the nineteenth century drew to a close, a quiet expectation began to grow in spiritual circles around the world. Many believed that such a teacher would soon appear.

After its founding, the Society's leaders travelled first to Bombay, present-day Mumbai, and then to Ceylon, now Sri Lanka, where they underwent Buddhist initiation. By 1882, the Society had established its international headquarters in India at Adyar, near Madras, present-day Chennai.

Within a few years, it grew into a worldwide movement, attracting seekers from many countries who were searching for deeper meaning in life.

Among those drawn to it were two remarkable figures, Annie Besant and Charles Webster Leadbeater. Their lives would soon become closely linked with that of the young boy Krishna.

Madame Blavatsky herself was widely regarded as a remarkable seer and occultist. Many believed that her life and work were guided by the Masters.

Through their guidance and her own profound insight, she was said to have access to esoteric truths found in the world's religions and in nature's hidden laws. She was among the first to gather and synthesise ancient wisdom, laying the foundations of modern Theosophical literature.

Her travels took her from Russia through Europe to India, Sri Lanka, and Tibet. She is said to have spent time in a remote monastery in Tibet in close contact with the Masters.

The formation of the Society also brought together many spiritually committed individuals who later became important writers and teachers. Through their work, these ideas continued to spread across the world.

Some of its teachings are especially striking. One such idea is that everything in the universe is alive, even what we usually think of as lifeless matter. According to this view, all forms exist at different stages of their own evolution.

It also teaches that life existed long before the Earth came into being and will continue to evolve elsewhere even after the Earth has completed its course.

Madame Blavatsky explained that this was not a religion that asked people to convert or believe blindly. She described it as a way of inquiry that encouraged careful thinking, questioning, and personal discovery. Students were encouraged not merely to accept ideas, but to examine them and test them in their own lives.

Soon, the lives of Annie Besant and C. W. Leadbeater, two of the most influential figures in this movement, would become closely intertwined with that of the young boy Krishna.

Two Great Theosophists

Two remarkable figures stood at the centre of the early Theosophical Society. Their lives would soon become closely intertwined with that of the young boy Krishna. They were Annie Besant and Charles Webster Leadbeater.

Both were born in the same year, 1847. Yet they met only much later, in 1890, at a Theosophical Society meeting in London. That meeting marked the beginning of a long and influential partnership.

The two were very different in temperament and outlook.

Leadbeater was known for his energy, courage, and strong personality. He also possessed unusual psychic abilities, including highly developed clairvoyance.

The word psychic is often used for someone who seems sensitive in unusual ways. Such a person may notice thoughts or feelings that others miss, or sense things that are not visible to ordinary sight. Leadbeater was believed to have such abilities.

Annie Besant, on the other hand, was a powerful leader and a gifted speaker. While Leadbeater was drawn to hidden and occult matters, she was drawn to people, ideas, and social causes.

In the early years of the Society, they worked closely together. Annie Besant had once shown signs of strong psychic sensitivity. She learnt these abilities easily and could have developed them much further. However, she chose to focus her energy elsewhere. Instead, she turned her full attention to philosophy, education, and social reform.

Because of this choice, Annie Besant often relied heavily on Leadbeater in matters of occult investigation. These concerned deeper and less visible aspects of life that cannot be understood through the senses alone. She trusted him deeply in such areas.

Leadbeater, in turn, had great respect for her leadership and intellect. Both believed they were guided by great spiritual teachers, whom Theosophy called Masters.

Annie Besant's path to Theosophy began in an unexpected way.

After founding the Theosophical Society, Madame Blavatsky published two important works, *Isis Unveiled* (1877) and *The Secret Doctrine* (1888). At that time, a well-known journalist named W. T. Stead was the editor of a popular magazine in London. Though he was not yet a Theosophist, he knew Annie Besant as a fearless thinker and writer. He asked her to review *The Secret Doctrine.*

As Annie Besant read the book, something unexpected happened. She found that Theosophy did not attack religion or demand blind belief. Instead, it offered a deeper and more thoughtful way of understanding spiritual ideas.

Questions that had troubled her for years now seemed to have answers. What she read moved her deeply.

In 1888, she met Madame Blavatsky. Like many others, she was struck by Blavatsky's powerful personality and depth of knowledge. Before long, she joined the Theosophical Society and became one of her closest students.

In 1893, Annie Besant travelled to India, possibly at Madame Blavatsky's suggestion. The country soon became her spiritual home. For the next forty years, she lived and worked there with great dedication.

She cared deeply about human freedom and justice. As a British woman who openly supported Indian self-rule, she soon drew the attention and displeasure of the British authorities. Yet she remained fearless and committed to her ideals.

After the death of Colonel Olcott in 1907, Annie Besant became the President of the Theosophical Society. The Society believed that this was not only Olcott's personal wish, but also in accordance with guidance from the Masters.

From that moment onward, Annie Besant stood at the centre of the Theosophical movement. Under her leadership, events would soon unfold that would lead to the discovery of a young boy named Krishnamurti.

Charles Webster Leadbeater was born in England in 1847. His father worked on railway projects in South America. As a boy, Leadbeater spent several years in Brazil.

Those early years left a deep impression on him. He travelled widely, saw unfamiliar lands, and encountered unfamiliar traditions and rituals that were not usually spoken about openly.

In later years, he described some of what he had seen. He said that certain rituals, which he connected with the Incas, reminded him of those of the Freemasons.

The Freemasons are a long-standing group known for their symbolic and often secret ceremonies.

These experiences filled him with a sense of adventure and mystery.

One journey, however, ended in tragedy. During a trip into the interior of Brazil, Leadbeater's younger brother Gerald, a boy barely seven years old, was killed by bandits. The loss affected him deeply and remained with him throughout his life.

Soon afterwards, the family returned to England. Not long later, Leadbeater's father died of illness. The family lost its main source of support and security. When a major London bank collapsed, the investments his father had made were wiped out, leaving them suddenly poor.

Leadbeater had just entered a college at Oxford University when this happened. He was forced to leave his studies and face a difficult future.

After some years of hardship, he joined the Church of England. He became a priest and served quietly in parish life. Yet even then, his interests lay elsewhere.

From boyhood, Leadbeater had been unusually sensitive. He felt drawn to hidden and unseen aspects of life. When he read books on Theosophy, something in them spoke deeply to him. He joined the Theosophical Society in 1883.

Soon after, he met Madame Blavatsky and was drawn to her. She recognised his abilities and accepted him as her student. Under her influence, Leadbeater left the Church, adopted a simple way of life, and travelled with her to India and Sri Lanka. There, he formally embraced Buddhism.

For several years, he lived in Sri Lanka, where he taught poor Buddhist boys in a school founded by the Theosophical Society. Later, he returned to England to tutor two boys. With him came a young student from Sri Lanka named C. Jinarajadasa, whom everyone called Raja.

Leadbeater came to believe that Raja was the rebirth of his younger brother, Gerald, who had died many years earlier. This belief mattered deeply to him, and he felt that fate had brought them together again.

Jinarajadasa accepted this belief and grew very close to Leadbeater. He admired his clarity of thought and his unusual abilities, and remained loyal to him throughout his life.

Leadbeater was known among Theosophists for his strong personality and his exceptional psychic powers. He was said to be able to examine past lives and hidden dimensions of existence. Whether people accepted these claims or not, many trusted him deeply. His influence within the Theosophical Society was considerable.

It was this influence that would soon lead him toward an unexpected encounter. It would change the course of many lives.

In February 1909, Leadbeater arrived in India. He came to work at the headquarters of the Theosophical Society at Adyar. He did not know that something far more important lay ahead.

He lived within the large, peaceful grounds of the Society. His home was an unusual octagonal bungalow on the eastern side of the main building. The place was quiet, shaded by trees, and close to the river.

Most of his work was ordinary. Letters arrived daily from many parts of the world, and Leadbeater spent long hours replying to them.

Leadbeater did not live alone. In the next room was Johann van Manen, a young Dutchman who worked as his secretary. Another resident of the bungalow was Ernest Wood, a young Englishman from Manchester.

Wood first became interested in Theosophy after hearing Annie Besant speak in England. When she became President of the Society, he followed her to India in 1908 to help with her work.

Another resident of the bungalow was Subramanyam Aiyar. He was the Vice-President of the Theosophical Society and a former judge of the Madras High Court. After retiring, he chose to devote his life fully to the Society.

Subramanyam Aiyar was also a close friend of Narayaniah, the father of Krishna.

Discovery of Krishnamurti

Narayaniah had joined the Theosophical Society many years earlier, in 1882. He was an active member of the Society and also belonged to its Esoteric Section, where only long-standing and trusted members were admitted. He had even hosted Society meetings at his home in Madanapalle.

At that time, neither Narayaniah nor anyone else could have guessed that one of the boys in his family would soon attract worldwide attention.

After his retirement in 1909, Narayaniah found himself with little to do. He was only fifty-two and still eager to serve the Society. He wrote to Annie Besant, offering to work full-time. In his letter, he explained that he was a widower living with his four sons. He asked if he might serve the Society in return for accommodation at Adyar.

Annie Besant did not know him personally, and at first his request was turned down. A little later, however, one of the Society's secretaries needed an assistant. Narayaniah's name was suggested, and this time he was accepted.

In January 1909, Narayaniah moved to Adyar with his four sons and a nephew. Since there was no room within the compound, they settled in an old cottage just outside the gates. Narayaniah's sister came to live with them and managed the household and cooking.

The nearest school was three miles away, at Mylapore. Krishna, Nitya, and their cousin were admitted there. Every day, the boys walked the three miles to and from school.

Sivaram, the eldest, joined Presidency College in Madras. Sadananda remained at home because of his disability and could not attend school.

In the evenings, Krishna and Nitya often visited Subramanyam Aiyar at the bungalow to do their homework. Ernest Wood would usually join them and help with their lessons.

The Adyar River flowed calmly behind the bungalow. Beyond it lay a long stretch of private beach. Many evenings, Subramanyam and others went there for a swim. Krishna and Nitya often went along and sat quietly on the sand, watching them swim.

One evening, Leadbeater was also on the beach. Something there caught his attention.

He noticed two boys who stood out clearly against the background of the shore. On returning to the bungalow, he spoke to Ernest Wood about it.

One of the boys, he said, had an aura unlike any he had ever seen. It showed not a trace of selfishness.

Leadbeater was known as a clairvoyant and was believed to see the auras of people.

Wood was astonished to hear that Leadbeater was talking about Krishna. He had known the boy as a dull and absent-minded child who came to him daily for help with his homework.

That did not change Leadbeater's view. He said that the boy would one day become a great spiritual teacher and an inspiring speaker.

To anyone watching, Krishna looked nothing like a child meant for greatness. He was thin and undernourished. His clothes were untidy. The front of his head was shaved, as was customary, with a long pigtail falling down his back. His teeth were uneven. His ribs showed clearly beneath his skin.

He suffered from a constant cough. His face often appeared blank and absent, as though his thoughts were far away.

Only his eyes were different. They were large, deep, and strangely still, with a quiet softness that was difficult to explain. Everything else about the boy seemed ordinary, even fragile.

Yet none of this troubled Leadbeater. He was certain of what he believed he had seen. Outward appearances, he knew, could be misleading. What mattered was what lay within.

Soon after, Leadbeater spoke to the others living in the octagonal bungalow. He told them something remarkable. He said that the Masters, Master Koot Hoomi and Master Djwal Kul, had spoken to him about the boys.

According to Leadbeater, the Master's message was simple and clear. They told him that the boys were special. They had been guided to Adyar for a reason and were now in the right place. If they were trained with care, the Master said, the elder boy would one day have important work to do for the world.

Leadbeater did not doubt this. What he believed he had seen in the boy, others would one day come to see as well.

This was how Krishna was discovered by the Theosophists at Adyar.

No one knows the exact date. It happened sometime before June 1909. When a man named Dick Clarke came to work for the Society that month, the discovery had already taken place.

Yet nothing about Krishna seemed to change. He looked the same as before, quiet, thin, and often ill. He struggled in school and appeared slow.

Many saw him as dull, without promise. Later in life, he himself said that in those early years he had been thought of as almost 'moronic.'

Only Leadbeater saw something different. He believed that something rare lay hidden beneath the boy's ordinary appearance.

The others in the bungalow knew only what Leadbeater told them. To their eyes, Krishna was just a weak and unremarkable child.

None of them could yet imagine that this seemingly dull boy would one day grow into a teacher who would deeply influence the thinking of people around the world.

The Lives of Alcyone

What followed would take the story in an unexpected direction.

To an ordinary passer-by, the boys might have looked like street children. They wore loose, untidy dhotis, their thin bodies bare above the waist. Dust clung to their skin. They appeared frail and poorly cared for.

This made Leadbeater's interest in them all the more surprising. He was a man who cared deeply about cleanliness and order. He was careful, even fastidious, in his habits.

Yet he felt drawn to these unkempt and sickly boys. Something about them held his attention, though he could not easily explain why.

An opportunity soon came for Leadbeater to see the boys more closely. Narayaniah invited him to his home for Nitya's sacred thread ceremony. The ceremony had been delayed because of his mother's death.

Such ceremonies are usually large family gatherings. But Narayaniah was now living far from his relatives, so he invited friends from the Theosophical Society instead.

Leadbeater had little interest in Hindu rituals. Normally, he would have been the last person to visit a modest Indian home for such a ceremony.

But Narayaniah had become important to him because of the boys, and so he agreed to attend.

Everyone's attention was on Nitya during the long ceremony. But Leadbeater kept his eyes on Krishna. He watched him closely.

Something about the boy seemed to draw him in. Leadbeater asked Narayaniah to bring Krishna to the octagonal bungalow the very next day.

Narayaniah agreed without hesitation. In those days, many Indians held Englishmen in high regard, especially those connected with respected institutions. Leadbeater was a well-known Theosophist from England and was now taking a personal interest in his son.

On a day when Krishna did not have school, Narayaniah brought him to the octagonal bungalow to meet Leadbeater.

Leadbeater was not an ordinary psychic. He had been trained in clairvoyance and had taken part in many investigations that Theosophists believed explored hidden aspects of nature. Some of these studies dealt with invisible forms of matter and subtle levels of existence.

He was also said to have trained himself to read what Theosophy calls *akasha*.

The akasha is said to be a kind of universal memory of nature. It is believed to preserve a record of everything that has ever happened, even in long-lost history. Leadbeater claimed that he could look into these records and trace the past lives of those he studied.

A few years earlier, he had carried out similar investigations in Europe with Annie Besant, examining what they believed were the past lives of several people, including a young boy named Hubert.

Leadbeater sat on a sofa, with Krishna seated quietly beside him. He placed his hand gently on the boy's head and then closed his eyes. The room grew still.

What followed was no ordinary enquiry. He was looking into the hidden records of the boy's past lives.

As he sat there, he spoke aloud what he was seeing. He described scenes and events from what he believed to be a former life of Krishna. Narayaniah wrote down every word carefully in English as Leadbeater spoke.

Krishna himself did not understand what was being said. He had not yet learned English.

There could be no conversation because Leadbeater did not know Telugu, Krishna's mother tongue.

Leadbeater continued to speak without pause. He described a series of events that seemed clear and connected. He spoke without hesitation, as if he were describing something he could plainly see.

The enquiry did not end in a single sitting. It continued over the next few months, usually on Saturdays and Sundays, when Krishna did not have school.

Leadbeater explored not only Krishna's most recent past life, but many earlier ones as well. In the first few weeks, Narayaniah attended every sitting and carefully wrote down whatever Leadbeater said. Later, Ernest Wood was asked to take down his words in shorthand.

Krishna was given the name Alcyone, pronounced Al-see-oh-nee. The name comes from the brightest star in the Pleiades cluster.

Following the same people across many lives could easily become confusing. The same individual might appear again, sometimes as a man, sometimes as a woman, and under different names in different places.

To avoid confusion, Leadbeater gave each person a new name. These were not ordinary names, but names drawn from stars, constellations, and Greek mythology. This made it possible to follow the same individuals across many lifetimes.

The stories revealed something unusual. A person could be born in very different forms from one life to another.

Friendships could turn into rivalries. Enemies could become friends. Relationships could change completely from one life to the next.

Annie Besant was given the name Heracles. Leadbeater called himself Sirius. Madame Blavatsky appeared as Vajra, and Colonel Olcott as Ulysses.

Mary Russak became Helios. Hubert was Orion, and Nitya was Mizar. Even Krishna's parents were given such names. His mother, Sanjeevamma, was Omega, and his father, Narayaniah, was Antares.

Some well-known figures from history also appeared. Julius Caesar was named Corona, and Plato was called Pallas.

Through these names, Leadbeater tried to show a pattern. The same inner selves could be followed as they moved through different bodies, countries, and centuries, yet remained recognisable in character.

By November, Leadbeater had already examined twenty past lives. Early the next year, he explored ten more. This brought the total to thirty lives. They were studied in reverse order, moving steadily backward in time.

The life stories stretched from 624 A.D. back to 22,662 B.C., covering a vast span of time.

They were said to show how destinies crossed, separated, and met again across many births. The life stories were presented as detailed and interconnected.

Leadbeater was known as a gifted storyteller. Yet the scale, detail, and continuity of these accounts went far beyond ordinary storytelling. For many readers, they seemed too elaborate and connected to be mere invention.

There were nearly two hundred characters in all. Each had clear traits, relationships, and turning points that carried over from one life to another.

Leadbeater dictated the stories almost without pause, and the narrative remained consistent throughout.

Later, Leadbeater investigated eighteen more lives, reaching back as far as 70,000 B.C. This was a time so distant that such accounts may seem difficult to imagine today. In all, forty-eight lives of Alcyone were examined. Six were drawn from very ancient times. The remaining forty-two formed an unbroken sequence beginning around 32,064 B.C.

These lives were later published in book form by Leadbeater and Annie Besant. The book was titled *Lives of Alcyone*.

At this time, Annie Besant was travelling in Europe. She knew nothing of what was unfolding at Adyar.

As Leadbeater completed the accounts of the thirty lives, he sent his notes to her. For several months, however, she did not realise who the central figure, Alcyone, really was. Even when the first papers reached her, she did not know that Alcyone was the boy, Krishna.

She learned of the discovery only in early October 1909 when someone at Adyar wrote to her with the details.

Finally, on 6 October 1909, Leadbeater wrote to Annie Besant again.

This time, he told her plainly that Alcyone was none other than Krishna, the son of Narayaniah.

In the same letter, he asked for her permission to move the family into a vacant house within the compound. The house needed only a few repairs.

Soon, Krishna's life at Adyar would change completely.

The Merciless School Teacher

School was a difficult place for Krishna.

He did not enjoy book learning, and lessons did not come easily to him.

Classes were taught in Tamil and English, languages he barely understood. His teacher did not seem to notice what he knew or how he felt.

His teacher showed little patience. Almost every day, Krishna was punished for failing to remember his lessons. He was beaten with a cane, called 'stupid', and sent out of the classroom to stand alone in tears.

When scolding another child, the teacher would suddenly remember Krishna standing outside and then call him back in.

There were days when Krishna stood outside for hours. At the end of the day, his younger brother Nitya would quietly take his hand and walk him home.

Before long, word of the teacher's harsh treatment reached the Theosophists living in the octagonal bungalow. When Leadbeater heard what was happening, he was deeply disturbed.

He told Dick Clarke what the Master had said about the school teacher. He had remarked that the man should be selling bootlaces in the streets instead of teaching children.

The Master had made it clear that the boys had to be taken out of this harsh way of living. Their food had to change. Their bodies had to grow stronger.

They had to learn better habits of care and cleanliness. Above all, they had to be removed from a school where beating and humiliation had replaced teaching.

The caning only grew worse. In October, Krishna was beaten very badly. Leadbeater was furious when he heard about it. He insisted that the boys be taken out of school at once.

This was a painful decision for Narayaniah. Leaving a government school meant giving up formal education.

He worried about their future.

Annie Besant reassured him. She promised to take responsibility for their education and later arrange for their schooling in England.

Until then, the boys would be taught at home.

And so, quietly and without ceremony, Krishna's days of regular school came to an end.

The Unusual School

With the boys withdrawn from school, the Theosophical Society compound became a school of an unusual kind. There were no classrooms and no examinations. Learning took place through living, watching, listening, and quiet guidance.

Krishna refused to study alone. He would not accept any training unless Nitya sat beside him. Even the simplest lesson was turned down if his brother was excluded. In the end, it was decided that both boys would be taught together.

The small group of Theosophists in the octagonal bungalow, people from different countries and cultures, soon became the boys' teachers. Each taught in his own way.

They had heard from Ernest Wood that Leadbeater had spoken of instructions received from the Masters. These were directions to prepare Krishna to serve as the human vehicle for a great spiritual teacher, the coming Messiah.

Some leaders of the Society believed that the time had come for a great spiritual Being, known in Theosophy as Lord Maitreya, to bring a new message to the world.

In Theosophical teaching, Lord Maitreya is regarded as a Mighty Adept who has appeared in different ages to guide humanity. Many believed that this same Being had appeared in the past to guide mankind, first as Sri Krishna in India and later as the Christ in Palestine.

For this reason, when Annie Besant spoke publicly about the coming World Teacher, she often referred to him as Krishna-Christ. At Adyar, it was felt to be a rare privilege to help prepare the boys for this role.

Soon, a small circle of tutors gathered around the boys. Subramanyam Aiyar, Dick Clarke, Ernest Wood, and Don Fabrizio Ruspoli took part.

Ruspoli was an Italian nobleman who had once served in the navy. He had given up a promising career to join the Society.

Leadbeater also joined the group of tutors. His interest lay especially in teaching on occult subjects. He spoke about the Masters and the early steps on what Theosophists called the Path of Discipleship.

The boys spoke only Telugu. They knew no English at all. The tutors felt this would soon have to change, especially so that Krishna could speak to Annie Besant when she arrived.

Among the Theosophists, it was understood that the World Teacher, if he were to help humanity, would need to work through human life and speak to people everywhere. And so, Dick Clarke was chosen to teach the boys English.

Russell Balfour Clarke, known to everyone as Dick, was a young Englishman trained as an engineer. He had recently completed his first professional posting in East Africa.

Even then, he felt drawn toward Theosophy. With youthful seriousness, he decided to give up his career and offer his services to the Society.

Dick had arrived in June on the very day of Nitya's thread ceremony. Within four or five months, he had become the boys' first private English tutor, a role he would always regard as the greatest honour of his life.

Dick also took responsibility for their grooming. This proved far harder than he had imagined.

The boys were in poor condition. Their hair was badly neglected, and even their eyebrows were affected by lice.

Krishna's long pigtail needed trimming. The shaved patch at the front of his head, customary for South Indian Brahmin boys, needed time to grow back. His teeth were crooked, and dental plates had to be fitted.

The boys were also introduced to Western methods of bathing and personal cleanliness. That was entirely new to them.

Krishna often carried a dull and vacant look. He would stand by the window with his mouth slightly open, staring at the sky.

Again and again, he was reminded to close it. Each time, the habit returned.

Leadbeater grew increasingly irritated with the habit. One day, unable to restrain himself, he slapped Krishna sharply on the chin. The habit stopped. From that moment onward, Krishna never felt the same warmth toward Leadbeater.

The boys rose every morning at five. After an early bath and puja, they walked to the octagonal bungalow. A strict routine now shaped their days.

They spent most of their waking hours inside the bungalow. They returned home only for their main meals and to sleep.

On arrival, they were given hot milk. This was followed by a long talk from Leadbeater on esoteric life and occult matters. Portraits of the Masters lined the walls. The boys were asked to learn their names and recognise their faces.

After this came outdoor exercises. Then another bath. Fresh clothes. And lessons with different tutors.

Cycling was compulsory. It was treated as discipline, not play. Within ten days of receiving new bicycles, Krishna had already ridden 143 miles. He became fearless on the road and showed surprising steadiness when faced with sudden danger.

Dick Clarke and Ruspoli usually accompanied the boys. At times, Leadbeater joined them too. Some rides were demanding. Once, they cycled all the way to Chengalpattu and back, nearly forty miles in a single day.

Leadbeater also set out to remove fear from the boys. He sometimes told them frightening stories. One day he noticed that the boys, especially Krishna, were avoiding a deep part of the water. When they returned after swimming, he told them to go back and find the frightening place.

Study, meals, exercise, and even play followed a fixed timetable. Very quickly, the boys learned the discipline of time.

The Other Boy

Krishna and Nitya were not the only boys who came to live at the octagonal bungalow. Another boy, Hubert van Hook, was also there. He was thirteen and had travelled from America with his mother.

Hubert's arrival was not by chance. Even before Krishna was noticed, Leadbeater and Annie Besant had identified Hubert as a possible earth-vehicle for the World Teacher. Acting on their guidance, his mother brought him to Adyar so that he could be trained.

Hubert was a bright and handsome boy from Chicago. His father, Dr Weller van Hook, was the General Secretary of the Theosophical Society in the United States. Leadbeater had first met Hubert during a lecture tour in 1907 and had been deeply impressed.

Hubert had travelled in Europe with Leadbeater. In Dresden, Annie Besant and Leadbeater examined Hubert's past lives together. Later, Leadbeater suggested that Hubert might be a suitable choice.

The idea stayed with her. During a lecture in Chicago in 1909, she spoke with certainty that the World Teacher would appear in the West. She urged Mrs van Hook to overcome every difficulty and bring Hubert to India. His training, she said, was essential.

Mother and son arrived at Adyar in November 1909 after a long and exhausting sea journey. India was entirely new to them, and they knew no one except the Theosophists they trusted. One can imagine their surprise when they learned that another boy, Krishna, had already been identified.

Hubert was very different from Krishna. He was aware of his importance, and it was natural that he felt displaced. Annie Besant, still in Europe, may also have felt troubled. She had persuaded Hubert's parents to bring him to India, and all she knew of Krishna had come to her through Leadbeater's letters.

Leadbeater later wrote that Krishna, not Hubert, had been chosen by the Master. Annie Besant accepted this, yet she still hoped Hubert might have a place. She suggested that the boys study together.

Krishna, Nitya, and Hubert lived and studied side by side. Hubert was capable and intelligent, but he could not help noticing the special attention Krishna received. He said little, but he felt it deeply.

Leadbeater imposed strict rules. Hubert was not to touch anything belonging to Krishna, not even his bicycle.

He believed that even objects could carry subtle influences. Krishna disliked being kept apart. But for Hubert, the hurt was sharper.

Hubert lived at Adyar for five years. Later, he returned to America, where he studied law and built a respectable life. Yet the memory of those years never fully left him. Mrs van Hook was hurt too, though she bore it quietly. She remained kind to Krishna and Nitya and treated them with warmth. Her quiet dignity spoke for itself.

At the Feet of the Master

Annie Besant met Krishna and Nitya for the first time on 27 November 1909, soon after her return from England. The brothers were waiting for her with flower garlands in their hands, eager and a little shy. In the Indian tradition, they prostrated themselves at her feet. Annie Besant lifted them up at once and embraced them warmly.

From that day, a close bond grew. Annie Besant became a deeply motherly presence in their lives. The boys followed her everywhere and sat quietly beside her on the floor during her talks, listening attentively.

During this time, Leadbeater continued to receive guidance about Krishna. While asleep, Krishna was taken in his astral body to Master Koot Hoomi for instruction. He was placed under training as a young disciple, at a stage called Probation.

Theosophy teaches that human beings possess not only a physical body but also subtler bodies that cannot be seen with the eyes. One of these is called the astral body. In sleep, the mind is said to function through this subtler body, though such experiences are rarely remembered when we awaken.

In Theosophy, Probation is regarded as a period of testing and preparation. When a person shows inner readiness, he is first observed and guided by the Masters.

It marks the quiet beginning of a long spiritual journey. Only later, if considered ready, is one accepted as a full Disciple of the Master.

Each morning, on waking, Krishna painstakingly wrote down what he remembered from the lessons during sleep. The notes were only a few short sentences, but they were very clear, even though his English was weak and writing was difficult for him. These notes came out remarkably well.

Soon after, Leadbeater received further instructions from the Masters. The notes were to be printed and would become Krishna's first offering to the world.

When a small book finally appeared to the world in 1910, it was titled *At the Feet of the Master*. The author's name was given as Alcyone, the name used for Krishna in the accounts of his past lives.

The book itself was tiny, almost like a small pocket book, and written in very simple language. Yet it made a deep impression. It spoke of four essential qualities, Discrimination, Desirelessness, Good Conduct, and

Love. Of these, love was the greatest. If there is sufficient love in one's heart, that alone can bring about all the other qualities.

Readers in many countries across the world were deeply moved by its simplicity and depth. It was translated into many languages and read around the world.

Many Theosophists believed that the first teaching of the new World Teacher had arrived.

However, not everyone agreed. Some doubted that a thirteen-year-old boy could have written such a marvellous book with great philosophical depth. But those who were present vouched for it. They had watched Krishna write each morning. His English tutor, Dick Clarke, confirmed it.

Dick Clarke maintained that the words were indeed Krishna's own words. He had seen him write them, morning after morning, without assistance.

Later, Annie Besant and C. W. Leadbeater wrote long commentaries on these notes. After every two or three sentences of the original text, they added pages of explanation. What appeared in a few lines seemed to contain meanings that could be explored for a lifetime.

These explanations were later brought together in a much larger book titled *Talks on the Path of Occultism*, which soon became an important work in Theosophical literature.

Krishna himself showed little interest in the book. He did not reread it or treasure it. For him, listening and learning were enough. Once the writing was finished, the rest did not matter to him.

The First Initiation

Krishna's time of Probation was very brief indeed. On New Year's Day in 1910, he was accepted as a Disciple, only a few months after his Probation. This was unusual. Even Leadbeater wondered how quickly it had happened.

On 11 January 1910, an unusual alignment of planets was noted by astrologers. G. E. Sutcliffe, an astrologer, had written an article in The Theosophist describing this combination as one that might symbolise the birth of a Christ. On that day, barely ten days after his Discipleship, Krishna was said to have passed his First Initiation.

In Theosophy, Initiation is described as a stage in the growth of inner awareness. Just as the body grows from childhood to maturity, consciousness too is believed to unfold in stages, like the steps of a ladder. At the higher levels stand the Adepts, wise beings said to guide humanity. The First Initiation is spoken of as the first step in a long spiritual journey. It indicates a readiness to learn more deeply and to live with greater understanding.

While Krishna's body rested in sleep, he was taken in his astral body to other planes of awareness. In that state he was brought before great Masters, including the World Teacher, Lord Maitreya. Questions were asked, and he was put to the test. He responded remarkably well. Then a solemn and symbolic ceremony followed in those subtle realms."

Leadbeater had carefully arranged for everything. With Annie Besant's permission, her room was used so that the boy could lie undisturbed. People were asked to keep watch outside in the stillness of the night and ensure complete quiet. They remained on guard through the night so that early visitors in the morning would not accidentally enter and disturb the boy.

The experience continued for more than one night. From time to time Krishna returned briefly to ordinary consciousness, and warm milk was given to him for nourishment. Leadbeater remained beside him throughout, watching over him and guiding the process.

For the Theosophists around him, this moment held deep significance. They believed that Krishna had now taken the first step on the Path of Initiation under the guidance of the Masters. It strengthened their conviction that he was being prepared for a great spiritual role in the future. Many years later, however, he would speak very differently about such spiritual stages.

What made this moment notable was that Annie Besant, who was in Varanasi while Krishna was in Adyar, was also said to have accompanied him in her subtle state during sleep. Later, she described the same experience in her own words in a letter posted the very next day. The two accounts, one by Krishna and the other by Annie Besant, were said to be very similar.

Among the Theosophists, this experience further deepened their belief in Krishna's spiritual progress. He was now widely regarded as having entered upon an important stage of inner development.

When Krishna returned to ordinary awareness, he felt calm and deeply responsible. He wrote simply in a letter to Annie Besant the next morning that he had "entered the stream" and must now live with care.

However, nothing outwardly changed. He looked the same and behaved as quietly as before. Yet those around him felt that something unseen but important had taken place.

Many elders now began addressing him as Krishnaji. This mark of respect carried little meaning for the young boy.

Legal Guardianship

Plans had long been made to move Narayaniah and his sons into the Adyar compound. A new house was being prepared. But events soon began to move in a different direction.

Those guiding Krishnaji's training felt that his upbringing required complete stability and care. Slowly, Krishnaji and Nitya began spending more time inside the octagonal bungalow. Their meals were taken there. Their lessons were held there. Their days were shaped more and more by the life of the Theosophical Society. This gradual change created tension.

Narayaniah felt that control over his sons' lives was slipping away. He disliked Leadbeater, and Leadbeater, in turn, disliked him. Narayaniah did not want him to have any influence over his sons. Misunderstandings grew, and trust slowly weakened.

Annie Besant watched the situation carefully. She feared that unless matters were settled early, serious conflict might soon arise. She also believed that Krishnaji's inner preparations needed steady guidance, and that Leadbeater's role in this was important.

At the same time, Narayaniah had begun to object strongly to Leadbeater's continued influence over his sons. This created a serious difficulty for Annie Besant. She felt that the training already underway should not be interrupted. After much thought, she chose to take legal guardianship. It was a difficult but necessary step.

This was painful for Narayaniah. It meant handing over the care of his sons to Annie Besant. Yet he trusted and respected her deeply. To reassure him, she promised that the guardianship would return to him if anything happened to her. After deep hesitation, Narayaniah agreed.

On 6 March 1910, he signed a document transferring the guardianship of Krishnaji and Nitya to Annie Besant.

From that day onward, she took full responsibility for their upbringing. To protect the boys from further uncertainty, she remained at Adyar for a long period, giving up her usual travels. It was a quiet personal sacrifice, made willingly for the boys.

The decision marked a turning point in Krishnaji's life. Childhood was slowly giving way to a life shaped by expectation and discipline, though no one yet knew where it would lead.

Soon after, another formal step followed. Annie Besant arranged for the family name to be recorded as Jiddu instead of Geddu, so that its pronunciation would be clearer in English. From then on, the brothers were called Jiddu Krishnamurti and Jiddu Nityananda, the names by which they would later be known to the world.

Father Regrets His Decision

For a time, life settled into a gentle rhythm.

Krishnaji and Nitya lived happily with Annie Besant at Adyar. Every morning, she read to them for nearly an hour. They travelled through stories such as *The Jungle Book*, *Captains Courageous*, *The Scarlet Pimpernel*, and even Shakespeare. Their days were filled with bicycle rides, swimming, and quiet companionship.

But the calm did not last.

Annie Besant could not remain in one place for long. After nearly a year with the boys, she had to leave Adyar for a time. With her absence, old tensions returned.

Rumours began to spread again. Narayaniah's friends warned him that his sons were losing their caste and being shaped by foreign ways. His long-held distrust of Leadbeater deepened. Doubt slowly took root. He began to regret the decision he had once agreed to.

Alarmed by the growing hostility, Leadbeater wrote urgently to Annie Besant. He said he had received guidance from his Master. The boys, the Master had told him, had known hardship for long enough. Now they must be surrounded by order, care, cleanliness, and affection. Their bodies were to be strengthened, their habits refined, and their lives protected from fear and confusion.

Yet Leadbeater's manner only worsened matters.

He was firm and controlling, and often dismissive of Indian customs. When Krishnaji was to attend the shraddha ceremony for his late mother, a sacred family duty, Leadbeater brushed it aside as unnecessary.

Only after much pressure did he allow the boys to attend, and even then, briefly. This was deeply painful for Narayaniah.

Suspicion spread in the local community. What was unfamiliar was easily misunderstood, and misunderstanding soon led to fear. Narayaniah felt torn, grateful to Annie Besant, yet increasingly resentful of Leadbeater. The distance between father and sons quietly widened.

In September 1910, Annie Besant took Krishnaji and Nitya with her to Varanasi, where she had a house near the Central Hindu College she had founded earlier. It was their first journey beyond their home region.

They were now far from Adyar and far from their father. From this point onward, they saw little of Narayaniah.

The bond was not broken in anger, but slowly stretched thin by distance, misunderstanding, and regret.

Preparing for the World Teacher

Life in Varanasi brought another change for Krishnaji.

A small group of devoted Theosophists began gathering around him. They were much older, teachers, principals, and senior members of the Society. Yet they listened closely as he spoke about inner discipline and the qualities needed for a spiritual life.

Some felt they were witnessing something extraordinary. To many present, the scene brought to mind the story of the young Jesus in the Temple at Jerusalem, sitting among learned elders and astonishing them with his understanding. In a similar way, Krishna seemed to them to possess a depth that went beyond his age and schooling.

During these meetings, the group wore simple coloured shawls as a sign of membership. At first, they wore yellow silk shawls and were known as the Yellow Shawl Group.

Among the early members was George Arundale, the Principal of the Central Hindu College at Varanasi. As more people joined, the name changed to the Purple Order.

Krishnaji was named its Head, while Annie Besant and Leadbeater were called its Protectors. The group met quietly for study and meditation.

Despite this, Krishnaji's own life remained strict. His studies continued. His physical training remained demanding. His days followed a fixed routine. For relaxation, he was given a camera. Photography delighted him and brought him quiet joy, and in time he learned its workings patiently and took to it with great care.

Soon other organisations began forming around the expectation of the coming of the World Teacher. George Arundale formed one called the Order of the Rising Sun. It was founded on 11 January 1911, the anniversary of Krishnaji's First Initiation.

A few months later, Annie Besant and Leadbeater created yet another organisation called the Order of the Star in the East (OSE). This one, however, was different. It was an international body that gathered supporters from many countries and continued for many years. Members were encouraged to wear a small Silver Star badge so they could recognise one another anywhere in the world.

Krishnaji was made the Head of the Order, though others managed its work. A magazine was started, and branches soon appeared in many countries.

But not everyone agreed. Some Theosophists questioned why such organisations were needed at all. Protests followed, letters were written, and divisions appeared. In Europe, several groups broke away from the Society, including one led by Rudolf Steiner.

Krishnaji had not asked for these organisations, nor had he commanded them. He accepted whatever Annie Besant said and followed her guidance quietly.

For now, he was still a boy, carrying expectations far greater than he yet understood.

Grooming in England

By early 1911, Narayaniah had begun to regret giving up legal guardianship of his sons. A quiet fear had begun to trouble him.

Sensing this unease, Leadbeater urged that Krishnaji be taken to England for further education. He said this too was a direction from the Masters, who wished Krishnaji to be in England within six months. Annie Besant agreed. She believed England would shape the boys well and perhaps even lead them one day to Oxford, a name that carried great prestige for Narayaniah.

Before Narayaniah could change his mind, Annie Besant left for London with the boys in February 1911.

At first, only Krishnaji was meant to go. But he refused to be separated from Nitya. The brothers had lived, learned, and endured together. So, arrangements were made for both.

Their long earlobes were stitched, and they were dressed in European clothes. George Arundale left his post at the Central Hindu College to become their private tutor in England.

They sailed from Bombay on the ship *Mantua*. It was Krishnaji's first sea journey, and a difficult one. He suffered badly from seasickness, as did Annie Besant. Yet his curiosity never faded. He watched the ship closely, learned how its engines worked, and delighted the captain with his eager questions.

When they arrived in London on 5 May 1911, a group of Theosophists waited at Charing Cross station. Among them stood a sixty-three-year-old woman, Lady Emily Lutyens. She was the wife of the famous architect Sir Edwin Lutyens and the daughter of the 1st Earl of Lytton, who had once served as the Viceroy of India.

Lady Emily had only recently become a Theosophist after reading some of Annie Besant's books. Curious and thoughtful, she had come to the station simply to see the boy everyone was talking about. She did not know that this quiet meeting would mark the beginning of a bond that would deepen over time.

Her young daughter Mary, only three years old at the time, had not come with her that day. Many years later, she would become the chosen biographer of Krishnamurti, writing about his life with great care. But on that morning at Charing Cross, none of this could have been imagined.

The brothers were not introduced to Lady Emily at the station. Yet as the months passed, a strong affection grew between her and the boys. In time, Krishnaji came to regard Lady Emily with the tenderness of another mother.

Life in England was strict and demanding. Arundale taught them mathematics, Sanskrit, writing, and the works of Shakespeare. Physical training was compulsory. Gymnastics, riding, and long walks filled their days.

There was some time for play as well. The boys enjoyed simple games like croquet.

Krishnaji was put on an extremely strict diet, which he did not like. Leadbeater had laid down this unusual diet, believing it to be guided by the Masters, and Annie Besant ensured that it was strictly followed. She paid little attention to his dislike of it and made sure that he kept to it.

He was required to eat eggs, which were difficult for him because he had been brought up as a strict vegetarian. He was also made to eat porridge, which he disliked greatly. He would swallow it quickly with plenty of milk.

The diet caused him severe indigestion. He suffered from stomach pains at night and often slept poorly.

Annie Besant, however, remained firm. She believed the Master's instructions were important and did not allow exceptions. The boys had to give up the familiar, often spicy Indian food they loved. They were given plain meals that felt bland and tasteless to them. There was no break from this diet, not even for a day, during their four months in England.

The boys travelled with Annie Besant across Europe as she lectured. A powerful and widely admired speaker, her talks often drew large audiences. During their time in Paris, they attended several of these gatherings.

One lecture at the Sorbonne was about Giordano Bruno. He was a bold sixteenth-century philosopher who was condemned by the Roman Inquisition and burned at the stake in Rome in 1600. It was believed that Annie Besant herself had been Bruno in a past life, as described in *Lives of Alcyone*. This made her talk especially fascinating and drew large audiences.

The hall was packed with more than four thousand people, and many more stood outside. The atmosphere was charged with emotion, and Krishnaji later wrote that he had felt the presence of a Master there.

After four months, they returned to India in October 1911. Two months later, at the Theosophical Convention in Varanasi, something unexpected happened. Members of the Order of the Star were invited to come forward and receive their certificates from Krishnaji himself.

As this began, a powerful feeling filled the hall. People rose, wept, and fell at his feet. Some had not even brought certificates, but rushed forward, hoping for a blessing.

Krishnaji remained gentle and silent. He claimed no authority. The most moving moment came when Nitya stepped forward, prostrated himself, and fell at his brother's feet. The hall overflowed with emotion, not mockery but devotion.

From that day, Annie Besant and Leadbeater were convinced that the World Teacher had chosen Krishnaji as His vehicle.

Narayaniah had come and had seen it all. But he left the Convention silent and sullen, carrying a deep regret. He feared that his son might one day be ridiculed in his own country instead of respected.

A Father's Fear

By 1912, a quiet tension had begun to grow around Krishnaji and his brother Nitya.

Their father, Narayaniah, was growing uneasy. Friends and relations warned him that his sons were drifting away. Some said that the Theosophists now controlled their lives. Old rumours about Mr Leadbeater began to circulate again. Slowly, doubt crept in.

During this time, many events were unfolding around Krishnaji. After leaving India, he and Nitya travelled through England and parts of Europe with Annie Besant and other Theosophists. Eventually they stayed for several months in Taormina, a quiet town in Sicily.

It was there, on a full moon night in May 1912, that Krishnaji was said to have taken his Second Initiation. Those around him felt that he was being prepared step by step for a future spiritual role.

Annie Besant returned to London in early July to find a registered letter waiting for her from Narayaniah. In it, he demanded that the custody of his sons be returned to him and even set a deadline for the end of August.

This shocked many. Narayaniah admired Annie Besant and usually spoke to her with great respect. The harsh tone seemed unlike him.

When Annie Besant returned to Adyar, she called Narayaniah for a meeting. He said his real fear was not about her, but about Mr Leadbeater. He demanded that Leadbeater should have no contact with the boys, not even by letter.

Annie Besant knew this would be difficult. She believed Leadbeater played an important role in preparing Krishnaji for the future spoken of by the Masters. Still, she agreed in writing, hoping to calm Narayaniah's fears. A new legal document was signed. Quietly, she added another clause allowing her to take the boys to England for their education.

Soon after, plans were made for travel. Krishnaji and Nitya went to England and later to Europe, accompanied by trusted members of the Society. They were welcomed warmly wherever they went.

Around this time, Krishnaji began writing a small book on education titled Education as Service. He believed learning should grow from love and care, not fear. Teachers, he wrote, shaped young lives.

Yet one question remained. Who had the right to decide his future, his father, his guardians, or Krishnaji himself?

That question would soon move from letters into a courtroom.

The Court Case

Narayaniah's unease had now turned into open action. He demanded that his sons be returned to him by the end of August. His earlier patience was gone.

He had heard that Leadbeater was again in contact with the boys. Old fears returned. Friends warned him that if he did not act immediately, he might lose his sons forever.

Narayaniah loved his boys. Yet for years, others had taken many important decisions in their lives, including their schooling, their travel, and their daily care.

Encouraged by friends who opposed the Theosophists, Narayaniah took a public step. He wrote to newspapers criticising Annie Besant, Leadbeater, and the movement itself. What had once been private became public.

Annie Besant feared that the boys might be taken away by force and removed from her care.

Krishnaji and Nitya were moved to a quiet house in the English countryside. Their location was kept secret. A guard accompanied Krishnaji whenever he had to go out, even for visits to the dentist, as he was suffering from severe tooth pain. Nitya was unwell and had problems with his lungs. Their movement was limited for a time.

In India, the matter reached the courts. Narayaniah filed a case demanding that his sons be returned to him. At first, the accusations were serious. When asked to provide proof, he modified his claims.

Annie Besant chose to argue the case herself. A powerful speaker, experienced in public debate, she stood before the court without a lawyer and defended her position firmly. She said she had honoured her promises. The boys, she argued, were receiving the education that Narayaniah himself had once wished for them in England.

The court listened. Conditions were discussed and decisions delayed. At one stage, judgment went in Narayaniah's favour, and Annie Besant was ordered to return the boys. She appealed.

Krishnaji remained in England as the case continued. He felt deep gratitude and affection toward Annie Besant and clearly wished to remain with her rather than return to his father. Nitya, too, wished to remain with his brother.

The case moved slowly through the courts until it reached the Privy Council in England. During this time, Krishnaji turned eighteen and became legally an adult under Indian law. He was now free to decide for himself.

The long legal struggle came to an end. The boys remained with Annie Besant. Narayaniah had lost his sons, and there was nothing more left for him to fight for in court. In later years, he would see them only once more, briefly, before his death.

Growing Up in Europe

Krishnaji and Nitya spent nearly ten years in Europe during the court case. They moved often between different homes across England and Europe.

Lady Emily became very close to Krishnaji and cared for him with great affection. One summer by the sea in France brought rare happiness. Friends gathered. Mornings were filled with lessons, and afternoons with play and laughter.

Krishnaji enjoyed teasing younger girls and correcting their manners with playful seriousness. When the Star magazine, *The Herald of the Star*, faced financial trouble, he wrote asking for help. Support came mainly from Miss Dodge, a wealthy American supporter of Krishnaji and a friend of Lady Emily. She even offered him a house in London, which he politely refused. Money and possessions did not attract him.

Yet his life was carefully supervised. There was a strict instruction that two Initiates should always remain near him wherever he went.

These were Jinarajadasa (Raja) and George Arundale, both regarded as Initiates, who stayed close to him at all times.

This careful watchfulness was said to come from the Masters themselves. No explanation was given, and few thought it proper to question it. Those around Krishnaji accepted the instruction and carried it out with care. The reason for such constant attendance remained unclear at the time, though it would become clearer a little later.

Then the First World War began. Some friends moved away. Later, Nitya left to prepare for studies at Oxford. For the first time, Krishnaji found himself alone.

In his inner life, he felt a strong closeness to the Buddha. On one occasion, he quietly said that the Buddha was present in the room.

On the Isle of Wight, during long walks with Lady Emily, he spoke of fairies along the path. He seemed surprised that she could not see them. He was even more surprised to learn that most people did not believe such beings existed. He had seen fairies since childhood, and they seemed a natural part of the world around him.

The brothers became close to Jamnadas Dwarkadas, a warm-hearted cotton merchant from India. Jamnadas and Nitya grew particularly close. He introduced Nitya to horse-racing. Guided by what they believed to be a dream. They placed a bet and won.

Later, they travelled quietly to Manchester for another race and won again.

When Nitya returned late, Krishnaji was already anxious. Seeing him, he said that he looked unclean and should bathe. Later, when he learned about the gambling, he said, 'That is why you feel unclean. Many people must have lost for you to win.'

When Annie Besant heard that Nitya had used the winnings to buy a car, she arranged for it to be sold at once.

During these years in Europe, Krishnaji was quietly maturing in ways not always visible.

End of Formal Studies

Krishnaji had many practical abilities. He enjoyed understanding how machines worked, and had a natural feel for machinery. Cars especially fascinated him, and his knowledge of them often surprised those around him.

Academic studies, however, were difficult for him.

He struggled with book learning. He found it hard to remember what he read and showed little interest in examinations. He could not easily repeat information from memory. After years of tutoring, he failed his matriculation examinations more than once.

His brother Nitya was very different. He passed his exams with ease and distinction and was preparing to become a barrister. The contrast between the brothers was clear.

Their private tutor, Mr Sanger, was often disappointed with Krishnaji. Yet he noticed something important. Nitya had a sharper mind and a stronger memory, but Krishnaji's mind seemed bigger. He often grasped a subject more widely than Nitya. His difficulty was not only a poor bookish memory, but also difficulty in putting his thoughts into words.

During these years, Krishnaji was also gradually distancing himself from Theosophy and the Order of the Star. He no longer felt inwardly committed to them. Yet his affection and gratitude towards Annie Besant remained deep. He did not openly express his doubts, as he did not wish to hurt her.

In the summer of 1919, Annie Besant met the brothers again after four years. She asked Krishnaji to preside over a Star meeting. Though he no longer believed in the movement in the same way, he agreed out of regard for her. At the same time, he told her that if he did not succeed in his examinations, he wished to move to France and learn French.

In January 1920, Nitya passed his law examination. That same month, Krishnaji sat for his matriculation again. For the third time, he was unable to complete his papers. As he sat in the examination hall, he found that he could not recall what he had studied. Feeling he had no chance of passing, he left the papers largely blank.

Soon after, he left for Paris to live there for a while and learn French. School education, as usually understood, had ended for him. But his learning continued in other ways.

A Change Within

In Paris, Krishnaji lived quietly during this period, staying with friends from the Theosophical circle. Nearby lived a French family, the de Manziarlys, whom he soon came to know well. Madame de Manziarly and her two young daughters welcomed him warmly, and he grew fond of them. Their simple and affectionate way of life made him feel at ease.

One day, while speaking with Madame de Manziarly, something unusual occurred. In the middle of the conversation, Krishnaji seemed to lose ordinary awareness for a moment. Later, it felt as though his mind had been taken away.

He dismissed it as heat and fatigue and did not speak of it further. Yet the incident remained with him.

In July 1920, Krishnaji went to live with the Manziarly family at Amphion, near Lake Geneva. Life there was quiet and gentle. He read to the children, played with them, and spent long hours walking or sitting alone.

One afternoon, while reading *The Buddha's Way of Virtue*, he came upon passages about freedom and walking without dependence on a teacher. As he read, he felt a sudden intensity and clarity. The words seemed deeply alive to him.

Krishnaji was modest and uncomfortable with praise. He had never regarded himself as exceptional. Yet from time to time, experiences arose within him that he could neither control nor fully explain.

Around this time, he learned that Raja, the same Jinarajadasa who had once travelled with Leadbeater, would soon come to England. This troubled him deeply. Raja remained devoted to ideas of spiritual ranks, initiations, ceremonies, and past lives.

He often spoke of these matters with quiet authority, recounting events from *Lives of Alcyone* and explaining what should or should not be done on the spiritual path. By now, Krishnaji no longer felt at ease with such ideas. Something in him had begun to move in a new direction.

His discomfort increased when he read *The Disciple*, a journal filled with discussions about Masters and Disciples. He felt that sacred ideas were being repeated in ways that felt formal and mechanical. In a letter, he wrote that he did not wish to belong to anything that caused him embarrassment. If he were ever to hold a position, it should arise from what he truly was, not from something given to him.

When Raja arrived, he brought with him a young Indian named Rajagopal. Close in age, Rajagopal soon became one of Krishnaji's closest companions and their friendship would continue for many years.

Illness followed. Nitya fell sick. Krishnaji suffered from bronchitis and was sent to Antibes to recover. During those quiet days of rest, he reflected deeply.

The ideas and beliefs that had once guided his life were no longer entirely convincing to him. Something within him was changing, though he could not yet describe it clearly.

Love Blossoms

Nitya had been unwell for some time. In May 1921, doctors finally discovered the cause. Tuberculosis had affected his left lung. For Krishnaji, the news was deeply troubling.

In the 1920s, tuberculosis was often fatal. There was no reliable cure. Nitya's hope of becoming a barrister suddenly ended.

Krishnaji brought Nitya to Paris and placed him under the care of Dr Paul Carton. Complete rest was advised. Krishnaji arranged for Nitya to stay in a quiet house near Paris. Later he took him to Villars in the Swiss Alps. It was hoped that the clear mountain air there would help his recovery. During this time, Krishnaji travelled to Holland and stayed with Baron Philip van Pallandt at Castle Eerde.

Castle Eerde was an old and peaceful estate surrounded by forests and lakes. No animals were hunted there. The atmosphere was quiet and reflective.

The Baron, unmarried and without heir, made an extraordinary gift. In 1921, he donated Castle Eerde and nearly five thousand acres of land for Krishnaji's work, keeping only two or three rooms for himself until his death. Unwilling to own property, Krishnaji immediately placed it in a Trust. Castle Eerde later became an international centre of the Order of the Star.

During the Star Camp at Castle Eerde in 1921, Krishnaji met Helen Knothe.

Helen was seventeen, lively and cheerful. She was the daughter of a prominent Dutch Theosophist and had come to Amsterdam to study the violin. During this time, Krishnaji experienced what may have been his only known romantic attachment.

They spent quiet days together, walking through woods and cycling along country paths. Away from formal gatherings, they were simply two young people enjoying each other's company.

One day, sitting together on the open moors, Krishnaji spoke to her of his feelings. He was shy and found it difficult to speak openly.

He told her of the three people he loved most, his brother Nitya, Annie Besant, whom he called Amma, and Lady Emily. Helen now belonged among them.

Their affection was sincere and gentle. There was no physical intimacy, yet the bond was deeply personal and meant a great deal to him.

Krishnaji knew he would soon leave Holland. Before departing, he found an opportunity to see Helen once more. Then they parted.

He wrote to her frequently. Over time, he sensed that her feelings were not as strong as his own, and this caused him pain. Even so, the experience left a lasting impression on him.

He also wrote to Lady Emily, speaking of what he had felt. Through this experience, he discovered a new depth of emotion within himself. It was love.

An Unexpected Honour

Nitya's health had improved steadily within a month. Madame de Manziarly, who had been caring for him, took him to a chest specialist. After a careful examination, the doctor said he was strong enough to travel by sea.

Soon after, the brothers set out for India. They sailed from Marseilles to Bombay and then by train to Adyar.

Annie Besant had built two simple rooms for them inside the Theosophical Society compound at Adyar. The rooms were close to the main headquarters, where she lived. Each had a small veranda looking out towards the river and the distant sea.

The brothers enjoyed the quiet surroundings. Krishnaji especially liked walking in the evenings through the palm groves in the setting sun, when the air had grown still.

They were still in India in December 1921 when the Prince of Wales visited the country. By then, the Central Hindu College at Varanasi, once guided by Annie Besant, had grown into a full university. It was now known as the Benares Hindu University.

On 13 December 1921, Krishnaji was invited there and awarded an honorary degree.

It was an unusual occasion. Krishnaji had not succeeded in formal school examinations, and academic study had always been difficult for him. Yet he was now receiving a university honour.

The following day, the University conferred an honorary doctorate on Annie Besant.

This meant far more to Krishnaji than his own degree. Annie Besant valued the degree greatly and cherished it for the rest of her life. Krishnaji shared her happiness.

In private, he called her Amma, meaning mother. From that time onward, he addressed her publicly as Dr Besant.

It was his way of expressing gratitude and respect.

The Last Meeting

Before the brothers travelled to India in 1921, it was Nitya who suggested that they should see their father.

They had not met him for nine long years. The court case and its bitterness had broken all ties. During that time, Narayaniah had received no word from his sons. After his break with Annie Besant, he no longer visited the Theosophical Society and relied on scraps of news from others. The brothers, too, had not written even once. For almost a decade, there had been silence.

Narayaniah was living in Triplicane, not far from Adyar. When he received a telegram saying his sons were coming, he wept with joy.

He asked his daughter-in-law Sharada, Sivaram's young wife, who lived with him, to prepare the dishes the boys had loved as children.

When the brothers arrived that evening, Sharada stood shyly on the verandah. She later remembered how striking Krishnaji looked. He was tall, radiant, and full of life, and walked quickly with a light step. Feeling embarrassed, she lowered her eyes.

Seeing her shyness, Krishnaji playfully covered his face with his hands, pretending not to see her. Nitya gently teased him, reminding him that she was naturally shy.

Narayaniah rose to greet his sons. Overcome with emotion, he embraced them and wept openly. The brothers touched his feet in reverence. Krishnaji then sat close beside him.

They spoke in English, as the brothers had forgotten their Telugu.

After the first rush of feeling, Narayaniah stepped away briefly. When he returned, he washed his feet, a simple habit he followed after using the washroom. It had nothing to do with the boys, and the feeling between them remained tender throughout the visit.

Sharada brought the sweets she had prepared with care. Krishnaji refused them gently. Nitya accepted only an orange. Words were few. Feelings were deep.

They stayed for only about half an hour. Before leaving, they spoke briefly of Annie Besant.

Over the next three days, the brothers visited again. Narayaniah wished to see them at the Theosophical Society compound, but Sivaram gently discouraged it.

That was the last time Narayaniah saw his sons. He died in February 1924 and never saw them again.

Storm in Australia

Krishnaji and his brother travelled from India to Australia in early 1922. They arrived in Sydney to a warm welcome from members of the Theosophical Society and the Order of the Star. Yet beneath the smiles, a serious conflict was already brewing.

Two senior leaders of the Society stood on opposite sides. One was C. W. Leadbeater, a powerful and influential figure who believed that Theosophy could work alongside church rituals. He held that spiritual growth could be recognised through ranks and Initiations.

The other was T. H. Martyn, the General Secretary of the Society in Australia, and head of its Esoteric Section. Martyn believed that Theosophy had drifted away from its original spirit. He called for a return to the simpler approach first associated with Madame Blavatsky, free of ceremonies and claims of spiritual rank.

Another figure stood close to Leadbeater in this dispute. He was James Ingall Wedgwood, a brilliant but flamboyant young man who had become both a Theosophist and a priest in the Liberal Catholic Church.

Wedgwood admired Leadbeater deeply, and the two often worked together.

In time, Wedgwood even consecrated Leadbeater as a bishop in the Liberal Catholic Church for Australasia. Years earlier, Leadbeater and Annie Besant had supported Wedgwood in becoming a bishop in the Church. Some people felt this later step was a curious exchange of favours between friends. Wedgwood explained that it had the blessing of Lord Maitreya, a name often invoked in such matters. Once such words were spoken, few felt able to question them.

At the heart of the dispute was authority. Who had the right to guide another person's inner life? Who could decide whether someone had reached a higher spiritual stage?

When the Australian Convention opened in April 1922, the disagreement burst into the open. Supporters on both sides spoke strongly. Voices rose. Old accusations were repeated. For more than two hours the meeting became heated and disorderly.

In the end, a vote of confidence was taken. The majority supported Leadbeater. Martyn walked out of the hall, and the division became permanent.

Krishnaji watched the events quietly. He was troubled. He found it hard to reconcile the language of truth and brotherhood with the anger he had witnessed. The struggle over spiritual authority disturbed him deeply.

Later he tried to speak with Martyn in a spirit of reconciliation. But their differences could not be resolved.

The conflict did not end with the Convention. Tensions remained high. Martyn was especially concerned about Leadbeater's close association with Wedgwood, whose earlier conduct had been surrounded by controversy and had raised doubts in Australia.

Believing that these matters should be examined openly, Martyn gathered documents and statements and shared them with influential people, and later with the press. What had begun as an internal dispute soon became public.

Newspapers began publishing reports daily. Many were careless or exaggerated. Serious issues were mixed with mockery and wild speculation.

The authorities felt obliged to respond. The Minister of Justice ordered a formal enquiry. It was not a criminal trial. Its purpose was to examine the claims and find out whether any misconduct had happened.

Krishnaji, Nitya, Raja, and several other boys voluntarily went to the police to answer questions.

The experience was distressing. Some questions were personal and uncomfortable. One of the boys was very young and did not fully understand what was being asked. Krishnaji found the situation painful. The enquiry concluded quickly, and no wrongdoing was established.

Even so, the public controversy continued. The press carried further criticism and ridicule. Theosophy, the

Masters, the Order of the Star, and several individuals were openly mocked.

The brothers themselves soon became objects of public curiosity. As Krishnaji walked through Sydney, strangers pointed at him. Some whispered; others laughed. He heard the word 'Messiah' spoken sarcastically. On one occasion someone called out, 'There goes that fellow with thirty lives.'

Krishnaji hoped to speak privately with Leadbeater, but this proved difficult. Leadbeater was often surrounded by devoted young boys who lived and studied with him. It was rarely possible to meet him alone. In such an atmosphere, rumours spread easily.

What troubled Krishnaji most was not only the criticism from outside, but the atmosphere of unquestioning loyalty he saw around certain leaders. He noticed how readily many people accepted guidance without examining it for themselves.

The weeks in Australia left a deep impression on him. He had seen how quickly ideals could give way to anger, and how easily spiritual authority could be defended or attacked.

Something within him had begun to question the very meaning of authority and organised spiritual life.

Across the Pacific

The long sea journey to Australia had affected Nitya's health. His cough worsened, and after the Sydney Convention doctors gave worrying news. Both lungs now appeared to be infected, and they advised that he leave Sydney at once for a cooler climate.

Nitya was taken to a quiet hotel in Katoomba in the Blue Mountains. Krishnaji remained with him, wanting to stay close and watch over his brother. The journey from Sydney was long, and travelling back and forth each day was tiring for him. By now their stay in Australia had extended far beyond what they had planned.

As plans were made for their journey home, Krishnaji was anxious about Nitya's condition. Travel through India or South Africa would involve intense heat. Doctors therefore advised another route. The brothers would return across the Pacific, sailing to San Francisco and then onward to Europe.

Help came from Mr Warrington, an American Theosophist who had come to Sydney for the Convention. He lived in a quiet valley in California called Ojai. He suggested that the brothers spend a few months there resting. A friend had offered them a house, and he believed the peaceful surroundings would help Nitya regain strength.

Krishnaji welcomed the proposal. He hoped the calm valley would restore Nitya's strength, and give him time for reading and quiet reflection. Annie Besant and Leadbeater approved the plan, and Annie Besant soon returned to India.

On 14 June 1922, Krishnaji and Nitya sailed for San Francisco with Warrington. Another American Theosophist, Fritz Kunz, joined them. Just before their departure, Leadbeater conveyed a message that he said came from the Master. It encouraged Krishnaji to grow inwardly, to be patient with differences, and to recognise even a small spark of truth in others.

During the long voyage, Krishnaji reflected on the message. At the same time, he felt increasingly uncomfortable with the devotion directed toward him. He began to question the role shaped around him.

The journey across the Pacific was largely uneventful. Some passengers were friendly and curious. Others were less welcoming. Krishnaji responded quietly to both.

In San Francisco, the brothers stayed briefly with a lady Theosophist who was a professor at Berkeley. She showed them the campus. Krishnaji observed that social divisions of caste and colour were less visible there than in some places he had known before. They also consulted a doctor regarding Nitya's health. The doctor suggested that the right lung might not be affected after all and that the climate of Ojai would likely suit him.

With cautious hope, the brothers prepared to travel inland to the quiet valley of Ojai.

Ojai

After two quiet nights in San Francisco, the brothers travelled south by train. On the morning of 6 July 1922, they reached Ventura. There, Mary Gray met them and drove them inland to the Ojai Valley.

Mrs Gray owned several small cottages among the groves in the valley. One was rented by Warrington. Two pine cottages stood empty, and she offered one to the brothers. A woman came each day to prepare breakfast and lunch, and in the evenings the brothers cooked for themselves.

Ojai, pronounced 'O-high', was simple and still. Orange and avocado groves surrounded the cottage. For the first time in many years, there were no formal schedules and no constant supervision. Life moved quietly.

The valley lay above sea level. Days were warm, the air dry and clear, and the nights cool. The brothers rode in the hills and bathed in a stream that flowed down the canyon. The setting seemed well suited for rest.

During these early weeks, they met Rosalind Williams, an eighteen-year-old friend of Mrs Gray who lived nearby. She had bright blue eyes and a cheerful manner. She soon became a regular visitor. She and Nitya grew close, and a quiet affection developed between them.

But the calm did not last. Nitya's health suddenly worsened. His cough became severe, and he began running a fever. Tests indicated that tuberculosis had spread to his kidney and spleen.

Rosalind asked her mother if she might stay and help nurse him. Her sister was a Theosophist, and the family was aware of the stories surrounding Krishnaji. Although tuberculosis was greatly feared at the time, her mother agreed. Rosalind remained, offering steady care and companionship during Nitya's illness.

Hope came from an unexpected source. A doctor in San Francisco, Dr Abrams, claimed to have developed a new electrical treatment for tuberculosis, which he called the 'Oscilloclast'. The machine sent mild vibrations through the body, which were believed to assist healing. The treatment was painless but required long hours of stillness.

Warrington arranged to hire one of these machines. Nitya spent many hours each day connected to it, enduring the exhausting routine. Krishnaji observed the device with interest, while Rosalind stayed nearby, giving encouragement.

Thus, life in Ojai continued quietly, marked by illness, care, and uncertainty.

The Process Begins

Ojai was quiet and peaceful. For the first time in many years, Krishnaji had privacy. There were no constant visitors and no fixed programmes. His days were largely his own.

Each morning and evening, he spent time in silence, reflecting on the message he had received in Sydney. He did not try to analyse it, but simply remained with it.

For several weeks, life continued without disturbance.

Then, on 17 August 1922, he began to feel unusually tired. The following morning he seemed better, but after breakfast the discomfort returned. He lay down to rest.

Soon his condition changed. His body began to tremble. He moaned in pain, clenched his fists, and appeared to be in intense discomfort. Those around him were alarmed. There was no sign of fever or of any known illness that could explain the symptoms.

Rosalind tried to assist him, but he asked not to be touched.

As the hours passed, he became extremely sensitive to sound. Even distant noises seemed to disturb him. He repeatedly asked for quiet. At times, he spoke as though people from Adyar were present.

By evening, the distress subsided. He was calm but exhausted. He ate little and slept deeply.

The next day, the pain returned and appeared more intense. It came in waves and then disappeared, leaving no visible sign. Those with him could not understand what was happening.

On the third day, Sunday, his condition seemed most severe.

He moved in and out of awareness. At moments he spoke clearly, asking why he had been brought so far from India.

He said more than once that he did not know where he was. At other times, he seemed overwhelmed by sensations that others could not perceive.

Later that evening, he became distressed by what he called 'dirt'. He complained about the bed, the room, and even the presence of others. He asked to go outside.

Uncertain how to help, those around him watched anxiously.

Eventually, he went out to the veranda and sat alone, holding a cushion and keeping some distance from the others. The light was fading, and the valley had grown quiet.

Warrington then suggested that he should sit beneath a young pepper tree.

At first, Krishnaji hesitated. Then he rose and walked toward it.

Under the Pepper Tree

Night had fallen.

Krishnaji sat beneath the pepper tree. Its thin leaves formed a dark canopy above him. At first, he spoke softly. Then he let out a deep sigh and wondered aloud why he had not been brought there earlier.

After days of little food, his voice was weak. He began to chant quietly a mantram he had sung each evening in the shrine room at Adyar. When the chant ended, there was silence. Those nearby later spoke of a deep stillness settling over the valley.

Krishnaji later wrote that his awareness changed at that moment. He no longer experienced himself as separate from what surrounded him.

A man repairing the road felt as though he were himself the man. The tool in the man's hand felt like himself. The stone, the dust, the tree, and the grass appeared part of a single living whole. He felt the wind moving through the tree as if it moved through his own body. He described sensing the ant on the ground and the bird in flight. Even a distant car seemed included in that field of awareness until it passed out of hearing.

Later that evening the pain returned. His body reacted violently, and the suffering was sometimes so intense that it left him trembling and exhausted. At times his consciousness seemed to withdraw and he fell unconscious while the body endured the agony. When the strain became too great, the body seemed almost to call him back, and the pain suddenly eased. He described slipping out of his body and seeing his physical form below. Above, he noticed a bright star. After some time, he returned quietly to the house.

In later years these episodes came to be known as 'the Process'.

On 3 September 1922 the episodes returned, this time far more intense. The suffering was so great that it was difficult even for those around him to watch. They came in the evenings, with burning heat, uncontrolled trembling like a malaria patient, and severe pain along the spine.

Nitya observed carefully and kept notes of the time, duration, and intensity of each episode. Seeking an explanation, he wondered whether the experience resembled what some traditions describe as Kundalini.

However, no clear conclusion was reached. The events did not fit neatly into any established category.

Over the following months and years similar episodes would recur intermittently.

Krishnaji rarely spoke about them in detail. When questioned, he usually avoided explanation.

What happened beneath the pepper tree in Ojai remained a matter of record, reflection, and differing interpretation.

Intelligence of the Process

From the beginning, Krishnaji seemed to accept the Process without resistance. It was as if he knew about it.

He never spoke of it to anyone, not even to those closest to him. Whatever it was, he treated it with seriousness. He did not complain or try to analyse it publicly. He allowed it to unfold, even when the pain was severe and unbearable. He bore the suffering quietly.

When the episodes began, the physical pain often became intense. He would toss restlessly on the bed or move about in distress, then suddenly fall to the floor with a crash. When he realised this was happening, he placed a cushion to break his fall. After a time of unbearable agony, he would lose his ordinary awareness while the body continued to bear the pain.

During these periods, his behaviour changed noticeably. His voice became softer and childlike. At times he addressed Rosalind as 'Mother', as though he were a small boy again. She was only a young woman, not his mother. He appeared to slip into an earlier state of memory, though in his normal life he remembered very little of his childhood.

Those present were puzzled by these changes.

Later, some interpreted this as the body responding independently when the pain became overwhelming. In Theosophical language, this was described as the 'body elemental', the natural life principle associated with the physical organism. In this state, the body endured the pain while a deeper level of awareness withdrew.

The Process seemed to follow a pattern. It often came at certain times of the day and sometimes seemed to follow a regular rhythm. When the pain became too severe, it would subside. After a period of rest, it would return again with greater vigour.

Strangely, Krishnaji seemed to know beforehand when an episode might begin again.

When the suffering ended for the day, he often remembered little of what had taken place. He would ask others how the body had suffered, and they would tell him.

Those around him struggled to understand what they were witnessing. The events did not fit easily into medical or spiritual categories.

In time, it became evident that the Process had a rhythm or order of its own. It always paused, as if with some compassion. Those caring for him found respite and time to have their meals in peace. The Process also stopped when there were visitors, as if it had an intelligence of its own. Whether this reflected the body's response, the mind's reaction, or something else was unknown.

What was clear was that the Process was not random. It followed patterns that repeated over months and years into Krishnaji's later life.

The Third Person: K

The events at Ojai marked a turning point in Krishnaji's life. Those close to him began to notice changes in him, though no one yet understood them.

Over the years, he had been called by different names. As a small boy, he was known simply as Krishna.

After the publication of *Lives of Alcyone*, some referred to him as Alcyone. Following his First Initiation, many began calling him Krishnaji, a name still used with affection in India.

Later in life, another change appeared. He often stopped referring to himself as "I." Instead, in conversation and letters, he sometimes spoke of himself in the third person and used only a single letter, K.

Not Mr K. Not Shri K. Not Swami or Bhagwan. Not even K-ji.

Simply K.

He did not present this as a formal decision or spiritual declaration. It was simply the way he spoke.

Observers have offered different interpretations. Some felt it reflected a change in his sense of identity. Others saw it as a practical way of avoiding personal emphasis.

When Mary Lutyens began writing his biography, *Krishnamurti: The Years of Awakening*, she discussed this usage with him. From the period following the events at Ojai, she referred to him as K, following his own manner of speech. From here on, we too will call him K.

The Pine Cottage

The Process seemed to follow a pattern. It often grew quiet when the moon was bright and began again as it waned. K seemed aware of when it might begin, but seldom spoke about it.

During this period, the woman who had been cooking for the brothers left, and Rosalind took on much of the daily responsibility. She cooked, cared for Nitya, and remained nearby whenever the Process returned. The strain was considerable.

On 25 September, the Process finally came to an end at Ojai, at least for a time.

The prolonged tension affected Nitya deeply. He watched his brother suffer while managing his own fragile health. It was exhausting. By the end of October, the brothers travelled to Hollywood to consult Dr Strong.

After examination, the doctor placed both under treatment. The sessions helped Nitya, and his strength gradually improved. K also benefited physically.

For the next two months, they stayed in Hollywood with Dr John Ingleman, a Swedish Theosophist known for strict dietary discipline. The brothers followed a severe diet. K accepted it without protest.

In December, they returned to Ojai. Not long afterward, the Process resumed, and the physical pain was again intense.

Early 1923 was also a period of activity for K. He worked for the Order of the Star and for the Theosophical Society. He wrote editorials, answered correspondence, and sent messages to groups in various countries. He gave public talks and addressed students in schools and colleges.

Mrs Mary Gray had rented the small Pine Cottage to the brothers without imagining its later importance. It was there that the strange and historic events of the Process had first unfolded beneath the pepper tree nearby. The quiet valley and the small cottage had now become deeply associated with what had taken place.

In February 1923, an opportunity arose to purchase the cottage, and K expressed a wish to buy it. He felt that the place should be preserved, because something important and special had happened there.

He did not personally possess the necessary funds. Contributions were made, largely from Miss Dodge. This helped the brothers acquire the cottage, along with about six acres of land in the Ojai Valley. The land included open ground and trees, giving the place a sense of quiet and seclusion.

K did not intend to own property privately. A Trust called the Brothers' Association was formed to hold the land. On the property stood a larger pine house, which K named Arya Vihara, meaning 'noble dwelling'. This was different from the smaller Pine Cottage where the Process had first taken place.

The small pine cottage remained on the grounds, close to the pepper tree. In later years, many would associate this place with the beginning of the Process.

Money

You might wonder how K managed his daily life. Where did the money come from? How did he live, travel, and even buy a place like the Pine Cottage, when he himself showed so little interest in money?

It was one of the quiet mysteries of his life. K never seemed to think about money. He did not plan for it, save it, or worry about the future. Yet when something was truly needed, money somehow appeared, often just enough, and often at the right time.

This did not happen only once. It was noticed again and again over the years. Funds came for travel, for land, for schools, and for printing books. Many people, moved by his work, offered help. In later years, some income also came from the sale of his talks and writings.

K did not manage these matters himself. Others took care of practical arrangements. Trusts or foundations were formed to hold money and property for specific purposes.

One steady source of personal support came from Miss Dodge, who gave him £500 each year from 1913 onward. She offered it quietly and without conditions. K accepted it with gratitude and treated it as his own simple allowance. The larger funds used for schools or organisations, he never regarded as his personal money.

To those watching, it sometimes seemed that K had an invisible bank. It never stored anything. It never failed to provide when there was a real need. When nothing was needed, nothing gathered around him.

Most people must think about money, earn it, and plan carefully for the future. K's way was different. He neither chased money nor turned it away. It came when it was needed and passed on when it was not.

There seemed to be a quiet flow in his life. When something was truly needed, it appeared. When it was not, nothing gathered around him. It was as if life itself was taking care of him. He moved with that flow, without effort, like a leaf carried gently by a stream.

A Hidden Transformation

Around this time, K and his brother Nitya were travelling widely across America, speaking at Star and Theosophical meetings. Many sensed a change in him. Though still gentle and unassuming, K spoke with greater clarity and authority.

The Process did not occur when he travelled or spoke. However, when they returned to Europe, it began again, though more briefly and less severely. K continued to suffer pain in his neck and spine.

After a period of rest in the Austrian Alps, the Process returned with force. Rosalind was not present, and Helen cared for him through long nights of suffering. During these episodes, he mistook Helen for his dead mother. This had happened earlier with Rosalind as well. At such times, he would take the woman caring for him as his mother.

When the Process worked on his eyes, K cried out uncontrollably. Nitya later the agony was like being forced to face the blazing desert sun with one's eyelids cut off. Those nearby could do little except watch and care for him.

Nitya strongly felt that unseen beings were around. He sensed Master Koot Hoomi and other Adepts. When the suffering ended for the day, it felt as though the real K was going out with them, and the body had to call him back.

Messages received during this period said that the work was extremely delicate and of great importance. One message said that this was an experiment being carried out for the first time in the world. Another warned that the body was now like a fresh vase just out of the mould. It was so fragile that even a slight disturbance might damage it. The work would then have to begin again and take a long time to repair. Those around him were asked to be careful with him.

Back in Ojai, the Process grew stronger. Night after night it continued. Doctors could not explain it, and even Leadbeater, though widely regarded as an authority, said he did not understand what was happening.

Concerned, Leadbeater arranged for Dr Mary Rocke, a trained doctor and also a Theosophist who knew K well, to come from Australia and observe him quietly. She was trusted in such matters and had both medical training and knowledge of occult ideas. Privately, Leadbeater wondered whether K might be losing his sanity, yet none of his own knowledge gave him an answer.

Dr Rocke watched carefully for several days, observing the Process each evening. It continued in her presence, yet she could find no clear medical explanation, nor did her knowledge of occult theory help. Later, K said he had known why she had come. He felt relieved that she had not thought them all mad.

In April 1924 the episodes ceased. A final message spoke of endurance, courage, and a great work accomplished that would benefit everyone in the end. What had taken place remained difficult to define.

Great Ones Are Near

After the long and painful months of the Process, K and his brother stayed quietly in Ojai until the full moon festival of Vesak had passed. The rest eased K's body. Nitya still needed care, as his lungs remained weak. Soon after, the brothers travelled to England, where they were warmly reunited with Annie Besant after almost two years.

Life soon became busy again. K travelled with her across Europe, attending meetings and camps of the Order of the Star. People noticed a change in him. His words were simpler now, but they carried a deeper strength. He no longer sounded as if he were repeating ideas. He spoke as if something alive was moving through him.

At one open air camp he told the listeners something important. Belief alone, he said, was not enough. What mattered was feeling, a fire within like the energy of love itself. Without this inner flame, spiritual life became dry and mechanical.

K took a short holiday with friends in the mountains at Pergine. They lived simply, walked through vineyards, played games, and laughed together. Each morning began with quiet sitting. After that, K would read aloud from *The Gospel of the Buddha*. It felt like a gentle pause, calm and nourishing.

But the pause did not last long.

One evening, after a walk in the pine forest, K returned unusually silent and joyful. That very night the Process began again, more suddenly and more strongly than before. It continued day after day. Those around him sensed that this was not random pain. It followed a rhythm. It stopped when the body could bear no more and returned only when it could. It was as though the Process knew its own limits.

A few days later K said quietly that something special would happen that night. When the Process ended, he told the small group around him something important. Lord Maitreya had been present for some time and had left a message for them. K said the message had come directly from Him and from no other Master.

Those with him felt that something profound was taking place within K. It was as though the presence he spoke of was drawing close to him, though the full meaning of this would become clear only in later years.

The next morning Nitya read the message aloud to those present.

The message was simple and striking, and its tone sounded very close to K's own later-life words. It spoke of serving without self-interest and of not searching far away for the sacred. "Do not look for the Great Ones," it said, "when they may be very near you". The message ended with a gentle reminder that what people seek may not be far away at all. The Great Ones may sometimes be nearer than we think.

Nitya Falls in Love

After leaving Pergine, the small group of friends travelled to Milan. They stayed only briefly, moving wherever the brothers went. From there, K and Nitya continued to Geneva, and then to Holland. There they completed the legal transfer of the Eerde estate. Once this work was done, the brothers, accompanied by Rajagopal, returned to London.

In London, they stayed with Lady De La Warr at her home in Buckingham Street. She was a close friend of Lady Emily and a constant companion of the wheelchair-bound Miss Dodge.

Soon after, the brothers went on to Paris. Rajagopal remained in London to begin the final year of his law degree at Cambridge. In Paris, Lady Emily joined K and Nitya with her daughters, Betty and Mary. They were also joined by Helen and Ruth. Ruth was a young English girl who had earlier lived in Leadbeater's household in Sydney.

This smaller group then travelled together to Venice. In early November, they boarded a ship for Bombay, accompanied by Rama Rao.

Rama Rao was a bright student from Mysore in India. He had run away from home to study at the Central Hindu College in Varanasi and was much admired by George Arundale. He later became a well-known Indian scientist.

Lady Emily was looking forward to a long-desired visit to Sydney. Money was tight, as preparations were underway for her elder daughter Ursula's wedding. Once again, Miss Dodge quietly helped by paying for Lady Emily's and the girls' return journey. Lady Emily managed both her daughter's marriage plans and her own spiritual journey. This displeased her husband, Edwin Lutyens, who had little patience for what he saw as her spiritual interests.

By now Mary was sixteen. During the long sea voyage, a gentle romance grew between her and Nitya. Mary had loved him for as long as she could remember. Their time together at Pergine had brought them closer. At last Nitya spoke openly of his feelings. He told her that she meant everything to him. Though he had once liked her elder sister, Betty, it was Mary who now held his heart.

For Mary, the voyage was filled with quiet happiness. Nitya was her first love, and every shared moment felt precious. She watched him closely, not knowing that time itself was already slipping away.

Two days before the ship reached Bombay, they stood together on deck and watched the sun sink into the sea. Almost casually, Nitya told her that he had coughed blood that morning.

Mary felt her heart tighten. Tears rose in her eyes as the glowing horizon faded into dusk. She did not yet know it, but a shadow had already begun to fall.

Rishi Valley School

The group arrived in Bombay to a grand and noisy welcome. Many people had gathered to receive them. They stayed at Ratansi's house, which quickly filled with visitors, voices, and constant movement.

Ratansi Morarji was a prominent Parsi industrialist and textile magnate in Bombay. He was also a wealthy supporter of the Theosophical movement and often hosted Krishnaji and his brother Nitya when they visited the city.

The brothers quickly changed into Indian clothes, as K often did on arriving in India. Mary, now deeply in love with Nitya, hoped for a few quiet moments with him. But it was almost impossible. Crowds surrounded them wherever they went. Unknown to K, Nitya had already coughed up blood during the journey. Mary carried this worry silently.

From Bombay, they travelled to Adyar. The de Manziarly family, who were also in India at the time, welcomed them warmly. K grew close to Sacha, their cheerful son who had lost a leg in the war. Despite his hardship, Sacha's spirit was light, and the two formed an easy friendship.

K and Annie Besant stayed inside the Theosophical Society compound, while the others lived nearby. Meals were shared, and the days were lively. Annie Besant took special care of the younger girls, who soon grew very fond of her.

Each morning, K held informal meetings in his room for friends and visitors. In the evenings, everyone played volleyball on the old tennis court. Yet beneath this cheerful routine, a quiet worry was growing. Nitya's health was failing, and K felt it deeply.

Despite his weakness, Nitya travelled with K and Annie Besant to the Theosophical Society Convention in Bombay that December. There, K gave a public talk titled *The Citizen as a Divine Agent*. He spoke simply about awareness, responsibility, and service.

Soon after, K visited his birthplace, Madanapalle. For years, he had carried a quiet dream. He wished to start a school that would educate the whole human being, not just train the mind. Now he began to search for the right place.

Near Madanapalle lay a beautiful valley among rocky hills. It was called Rishi Valley, after a nearby hill named Rishi Konda. Local tradition spoke of a rishi who once lived there and foretold that a great centre of learning would one day arise.

K chose land in the nearby Tettu Valley. A Trust was formed, and nearly 300 acres of land were bought. He named the place Rishi Valley.

In time, a quiet school grew there among nature. It became the first of eight schools K would later found. At its heart stood a vast banyan tree, nearly three hundred years old. It stood as a silent witness to a vision taking root, recalling an old story of a rishi spoken of long ago.

Nitya Will Get Well

Nitya was the person K loved most in the world. He could not imagine life without him. As Nitya's illness grew worse, K's worry deepened each day.

By January 1925, Nitya was very weak. He had to leave Adyar and go to the hill station of Ooty to rest. He stayed at Gulistan, a quiet bungalow among trees.

Gulistan had often been used by Annie Besant and Leadbeater as a quiet retreat away from the busy headquarters at Adyar. In that peaceful setting they had spent many hours guiding and training the two boys.

Because Ooty was cool and secluded, they could study, reflect, and speak freely about the future. Some early discussions about Krishnaji's work and the Order of the Star took place there. K himself was again going through the Process, but his own pain did not matter. His thoughts were always with Nitya.

One night, in October 1925, he had a powerful dream.

In a very intense dream, K found himself before his Master, pleading that his brother might be saved. The Master listened kindly but said the matter must be taken to Lord Maitreya.

K then turned to Lord Maitreya, the World Teacher in Theosophy, who many believed guided humanity. Again he pleaded. Lord Maitreya gently explained that healing was not His particular work and that he should go onward to the Maha-Chohan.

In Theosophical teaching, the Maha-Chohan is described as standing at the same lofty level of wisdom as Lord Maitreya, though His work is different. While the World Teacher guides humanity through compassion and teaching, the Maha-Chohan works through inner transformation. He is associated with Shiva in Hindu thought, the power of renewal and change.

In the dream K saw the Maha-Chohan seated in immense stillness and quiet majesty. Overcome with anguish, he fell before Him and declared that he would surrender all his happiness if only Nitya might recover.

The Maha-Chohan listened in silence. Then He gently assured him that Nitya would recover. K held deeply to that assurance. To K, the dream felt real. The Maha-Chohan had given His word. K felt certain that Nitya would be safe.

When K awoke, something within him had changed. The fear that had weighed on him for so long was gone. In its place was a deep calm and a quiet certainty. He trusted that promise completely and wrote at once to Annie Besant.

From that moment, he no longer felt anxious about Nitya. Whatever lay ahead, he believed that his brother would recover.

Slowly, something remarkable happened. Nitya's strength began to return. He was soon able to leave Ooty and travel again.

The journey ahead was still difficult, but K remained steady and untroubled. The Maha-Chohan had given His word, and for him that was enough.

A Turning Point in Australia

Soon after, K travelled to Australia to meet Leadbeater. Before reaching Sydney, the group travelled through Fremantle, Perth, Adelaide, and Melbourne. Star meetings had been arranged in each city, and people welcomed K with great expectation.

In several places, plots of land were offered for his future work. These were called Star Lands. Some believed that one day centres for the work of the World Teacher would be built there. Land was also dedicated in New South Wales, Queensland, and Tasmania. K accepted none of it for himself. He agreed only when the land was placed in Trusts.

When at last he reached Sydney, the convention was held in a large open-air amphitheatre overlooking Balmoral and the wide waters of Sydney Harbour. It was built specially for gatherings of the Star and shaped like an ancient Greek theatre. It could seat nearly two thousand people. Visitors came with great expectation to hear him speak.

In Sydney they stayed at The Manor, the large shared home where Leadbeater lived with followers from many countries. Life there was strict and orderly. Meals were taken in silence. Daily routines followed a fixed order.

Spiritual progress was marked by rituals, festivals, and ranks. People spoke eagerly of Masters, unseen beings, and hidden worlds. Special days, such as the full moon of Vesak, when spiritual advancement was believed to occur, were awaited with great excitement.

Leadbeater stood out in the crowd. Tall and striking, with snow-white hair and a flowing beard, he looked energetic despite his age. His bright eyes and lively manner made him seem younger than seventy-eight.

The Manor had become a small international community. Nearly fifty people lived there, drawn from many parts of the world. They believed that living close to Leadbeater would help their spiritual progress.

What troubled K most was not belief itself, but how tightly people held on to it. Titles, ranks, and claims of spiritual growth felt unreal to him. After ceremonies, people often congratulated themselves. K quietly wrote that real change could not be measured by labels. He said that calling oneself spiritual without inner change was like holding a cheque book with no money in the bank.

Meanwhile, Nitya's health grew worse. Doctors advised moving him to the cooler Blue Mountains. K travelled daily to be with him. By mid-June, permission was finally given for Nitya to return to Ojai.

The sea journey was hard. Nitya grew very weak as the days passed. Rosalind cared for him without rest while K watched anxiously. At one desperate moment Rosalind prayed deeply for his recovery. Soon after, Nitya's breathing eased and the fever passed.

K remained inwardly calm. The Maha-Chohan had given His word, and for him that was enough.

Strange Events at Huizen

Huizen, a quiet town near Ommen in Holland, had become a European centre of the Liberal Catholic Church. Wedgwood, now a Bishop, guided its activities there, and several priests lived in houses around the chapel. Visitors had begun to speak of Huizen as a place where unusual spiritual events seemed to be occuring.

Among those staying there was Oscar Köllerström, a young Dutch priest who had earlier studied under Leadbeater. Around the same time, George Arundale and his wife Rukmini arrived at Huizen after completing a long lecture tour around the world. They stayed in one of the houses connected with the Church.

Soon after their arrival, remarkable claims began to spread.

It was reported that several people had suddenly passed important Initiations. It was said that Oscar had taken the Third Initiation, George the Second, and Rukmini the First. Such stages were thought to require many lifetimes of effort. Yet at Huizen they seemed to happen very quickly.

George Arundale became the chief messenger of these developments. He sent urgent telegrams and letters to Annie Besant, asking her to come at once. According to him, extraordinary spiritual changes were taking place and many more were expected.

Annie Besant was travelling and giving lectures in several cities. She was in Marseilles and had promised to speak in London. It was impossible for her to cancel everything immediately and come to Huizen.

When she returned to London, she found letters from George waiting for her, describing astonishing events. Hidden spiritual powers, he reported, had awakened in several people. Oscar had become clairvoyant, and powerful inner energies known as kundalini, he said, had risen in Wedgwood and Rukmini.

The letters also spoke of messages from great Masters guiding these events. One even suggested that they might soon visit the castle of a mysterious Master in Hungary.

At the end of one letter came an unexpected request. George asked Annie Besant for permission to become a priest in the Liberal Catholic Church.

This troubled her greatly.

Annie Besant had always been cautious about Church affairs and sudden claims of spiritual greatness. She wrote back firmly advising George not to take such a step without Leadbeater's approval. She feared it might harm his work in India. Leadbeater, however, was in Australia, far away from Huizen. He had no idea what was happening.

But events in Huizen were moving too quickly.

Before Annie Besant could arrive, George had already been ordained as a priest.

More announcements followed. It was said that people had taken new Initiations and received messages from the Masters. Each new claim seemed more remarkable than the last.

Annie Besant decided she must go to Huizen herself. She cancelled several lectures and travelled there with Lady Emily, Miss Bright, Shiva Rao, and Rajagopal.

When she arrived, she found the atmosphere charged with excitement.

Most of the reports about Initiations and spiritual powers were coming from George Arundale or Wedgwood. The two men supported each other's statements, and the news spread rapidly among those gathered there.

Annie Besant felt uneasy. Yet she faced a difficulty. For many years she had set aside her own clairvoyant powers and no longer used them. Without that inner perception, she had little choice but to listen to others.

George was also one of the people she trusted most. She had worked closely with him for years and believed deeply in his sincerity. Because of this trust, it was hard for her to imagine that he could mislead her.

Soon another troubling event occurred.

Only days after becoming a priest, George was consecrated as a bishop. A telegram had been sent to Leadbeater asking for his approval. But before any reply arrived, George announced that permission had already been given 'on the astral plane'.

The ceremony went ahead.

While returning from the ceremony, a telegram arrived from Leadbeater strongly objecting to the consecration. But by then it was too late. The act could not be undone.

Annie Besant was deeply disturbed, though she said little publicly.

Meanwhile new instructions and messages continued to come. Some concerned daily habits and clothing. Others spoke of great spiritual futures awaiting certain people with the coming of the World Teacher. Excitement grew each day.

To many observers, Huizen seemed filled with visions, messages, and sudden spiritual promotions. People believed they were witnessing the beginning of a great spiritual movement preparing the way for the coming World Teacher.

But beneath the excitement confusion was also growing. Claims multiplied faster than anyone could examine. Annie Besant began to sense that something was not quite right. Yet events were moving too quickly.

Far away in Ojai, K knew nothing about the strange happenings at Huizen. His thoughts were fixed on only one thing, the illness of his beloved brother Nitya. While Huizen buzzed with visions and spiritual titles, K quietly wrote asking Annie Besant to send Rajagopal to help care for Nitya.

Rajagopal soon left Huizen for the long journey to Ojai.

Storm of Visions

After the events at Huizen, the group moved to Ommen for the next Star Camp. K was not there. He stayed away because Nitya was unwell. Still, the camp went ahead with great excitement.

On the night before it began, a dramatic announcement was made. Annie Besant said that Lord Maitreya had chosen twelve Apostles for His future work on Earth. The message had come to her through George, whom she trusted deeply. Ten names were read aloud, including Annie Besant, Leadbeater, Raja, Wedgwood, Lady Emily, Rukmini, Rajagopal, Nitya, and George. It was said that two names were still undecided.

K's name was not included. He was believed to be the future vehicle of the World Teacher and therefore beyond the Apostles.

That same night, a fierce storm broke out. Thunder and lightning lit the sky. A violent cyclone swept through the area. Nearby villages were damaged, but the Star Camp itself remained untouched. Many saw this as a powerful sign.

At the camp, Annie Besant spoke with passion about the coming World Teacher. She linked events in the life of Christ to stages of spiritual growth called Initiations. She declared that the Teacher had already chosen His vehicle and His Apostles. Many, she said, had reached the highest spiritual levels.

More announcements followed. People were told they had passed new Initiations. For some, it was two in a single night. They wrote these moments carefully in their diaries. They were thrilled by what they believed was their own spiritual progress.

Soon bigger plans were shared. Annie Besant planned to found a World Religion and a World University. Several centres would rise across the world, and leading roles were already assigned. Annie Besant herself was deeply engaged and took everything very seriously. The future seemed grand and unstoppable.

When the camp ended, the group returned to Huizen. There, an even more astonishing claim spread quietly. It was said that several leaders, including Annie Besant, Leadbeater, George, and even K, had passed the Fifth Initiation and become Adepts, beings who would never be born on Earth again.

K, far away and unaware of all this, was congratulated by telegram.

Spiritual Excitement at Its Peak

At Huizen and Ommen the atmosphere became charged with expectation. Announcements of new Initiations and spiritual ranks followed one another rapidly. Messages were said to come from great Masters, confirming honours, roles, and future destinies.

For many, it felt as if they were standing at the centre of a great spiritual drama. Storms, sudden emotions, and powerful inner feelings were taken as signs. Every coincidence seemed meaningful. Every message felt historic.

Most people accepted these revelations with deep trust. When respected leaders spoke with such certainty, doubt seemed unnecessary, even disloyal.

Yet K was not there.

In Ojai, far from all this, his days were filled with concern for Nitya's fragile health. He knew nothing of the declarations being made in Europe.

When a telegram arrived congratulating him on a great spiritual attainment, he felt puzzled. It did not match anything he experienced within himself.

He replied carefully. True spiritual growth, he said, must first be confirmed by those he trusted most.

Meanwhile the excitement in Europe continued to rise. Titles multiplied. Visions grew bolder. The language of certainty grew stronger each day.

The excitement had reached its peak.

But quietly, beneath it all, a few unspoken questions had begun to stir.

Questions that would soon change everything.

The Spell Begins to Break

When the excitement in Europe was at its height, the first doubts quietly appeared.

When Lady Emily returned to London, a letter from K was waiting for her. It was gentle, yet unsettling. He wrote of his deep unease about everything that had happened at Huizen.

From distant Sydney, Ernest Wood also wrote with concern. Leadbeater was disturbed by Annie Besant's letters describing sudden 'spiritual advancements.' He rejected the whole matter and warned quietly, 'I hope she does not wreck the Society.'

Meanwhile, Annie Besant, along with George, Rukmini, Wedgwood, and Oscar, set out on a secret journey to Hungary. They believed they were being guided to the hidden castle of a mysterious Adept known as 'the Master the Count.'

Lady Emily was thrilled. She arranged her visa and gathered the necessary money, eagerly waiting for instructions. But none came.

Days passed in confusion. The journey led nowhere. At last Annie Besant returned quietly to Huizen. The search had failed.

Shaken, she slipped back to London and resumed her lectures. She explained nothing to Lady Emily. She seemed stern and wounded. Perhaps she thought, dark forces had interfered. How else could so many sincere people have been misled?

K wrote to Annie Besant with great care. He did not wish to hurt her. He even said he was glad about the events and wished he had been there. But when she asked him to confirm what had happened, he replied gently that he remembered nothing. His mind, he said, was filled only with concern for Nitya's fragile health.

Annie Besant then asked him to come to England so they could travel together to India. He agreed, though reluctantly. Nitya's condition had improved slightly, and others were arranged to care for him in Ojai.

K arrived in England on 23 October. Lady Emily met him eagerly, but the journey to London was difficult. For the first time, he spoke plainly. He dismissed the Huizen claims and criticised how easily they had been believed.

Lady Emily was shocked. How could he deny what so many had regarded as sacred?

What troubled her even more was Rajagopal's silence. He behaved as though it had not been real. Yet he had been present at Huizen and had shared in the excitement. Now he seemed to turn away from it altogether.

Later she asked K why he had not spoken earlier.

"What would be the use?" he replied quietly. "They would only say dark powers had taken hold of me."

Something precious, he felt, had been made cheap.

And though few were ready to admit it, the spell had begun to break.

The Last Illusion

K sailed for India with Annie Besant and a small group of friends. They were travelling to attend the Jubilee Convention of the Theosophical Society in India. Their ship, *Ormuz*, left Europe and moved slowly eastward across the Mediterranean.

Before the voyage began, the group spent a few days in Rome. They stayed in a hotel and visited the ancient city. George Arundale and Rukmini joined them there before the journey continued. But the mood on the ship soon became strained.

By now many people knew that K had begun to doubt the strange 'revelations' that had come from Huizen. The followers of Wedgwood and George looked at him with cold disapproval. Some of the churchmen walked about the deck dressed in long purple robes, large crosses hanging on their chests, behaving as if they were officials of heaven.

At times they tried to frighten K. Messages, they said, had come from the Masters. The Maha-Chohan was displeased with K's disbelief. If he refused to recognise them as true Adepts, his own spiritual progress would suffer. They even hinted at something cruel. Nitya's life, they said, would be spared only if K obeyed them and accepted their authority.

But Nitya was far away in Ojai, and he was not well.

On the evening of 8 November 1925, a telegram reached the ship. Nitya had influenza. K was worried, but he still believed his brother would recover. For some time he had held firmly to the promise he believed he had received from the Maha-Chohan. Nitya was necessary for the work that lay ahead. The Masters would not allow him to die.

A few days later the ship stopped at Port Said. When K returned to the ship, he found another telegram from Nitya. It was short and brave, like Nitya himself. The illness, he wrote, had become more serious, and he asked K to pray for him.

K felt a tightening in his heart, yet he repeated the same assurance to himself again and again. Nitya would not die. He could not die. He would be protected.

On the night of 13 November, as the ship entered the Suez Canal during a violent storm, a telegram arrived with the news of Nitya's death. The message was unclear in parts, and the ship's officers held it back. It was given to Annie Besant the next morning, at breakfast. K, who always ate alone in his cabin, knew nothing of the terrible news.

Annie Besant was shaken and deeply troubled. For some time she hesitated, trying to gather the courage. At last she walked quietly to K's cabin and broke the news to him.

Something inside him shattered.

He loved Nitya more than anyone else in the world, and now he was gone. For days, he could not bear it. At night he wept and called out for Nitya, sometimes as he had in his childhood. He began to speak in Telugu, a language he had not spoken for years. It was as if something had been torn out of his life, leaving an emptiness he could not understand.

But something else had also broken. All the shining promises he had been asked to believe in, the messages, and the idea that unseen powers would always guide and protect them. That faith fell away. He was left alone with the truth of what had happened.

Yet slowly, beneath the grief, another movement began.

In the quiet days that followed, K thought again and again of the life he had shared with Nitya. They had loved simple things, long silences, drifting clouds, trees moving gently in the wind, and music. They had laughed together, sung songs together, and understood each other without many words. Even when they disagreed, it never lasted long. Their life together had been full of quiet happiness.

Now that life was gone. The dream had ended. He had to face it, without turning away.

Out of that sorrow, something new began to grow. He felt a deeper tenderness for human suffering. If people must go through such pain, he thought, perhaps they could pass through it without bitterness, without being broken by it.

By the time the ship reached Colombo, his tears had begun to dry. He spoke quietly of what had happened. A new vision, he said, was being born, like a flower pushing through hard earth.

He felt there is a beauty in life that cannot be destroyed by death. A happiness deeper than events. A strength that does not fade.

At the centre of it was a love that did not depend on the body, a love that could not be taken away.

When K reached India on 25 November, his face looked different. Friends saw a strange brightness in him. The loss of Nitya had not hardened him. It had burned away his last dependence on promises.

Something had fallen away. It was not only the stories of unseen powers and great beings, but his trust in them. What remained was simple, and strangely strong.

Truth, he felt, was not distant or supernatural. It was something very close, something deeply human, something that must be faced as it is.

Sorrow and Awakening

Nitya's death was a devastating blow for K. It shattered the last traces of belief he had carried, belief not only in the Masters, but in belief itself. He saw that truth cannot be discovered through belief however sacred it may seem. Sorrow, when faced without escape, became his greatest teacher.

Many years later, he spoke openly about this transformation. He said that during Nitya's illness, he stayed awake at night, watching the stars move across the sky, wondering whether they could save his brother. During the day, he watched the shadows of trees, silently asking them the same question. Nothing could protect Nitya.

Then something changed. He realised that life is one, though it appears in many forms. As long as he felt separate from his brother, he feared losing him. So he held on to prayers, hopes, and comforting ideas. But when he saw that the same life flowed through all beings, his grief ended. Sorrow, he said, brings understanding. To love others deeply, he felt, one must pass through sorrow. It was not cruelty, but a simple and truthful way of living.

In December 1925, Leadbeater arrived in Colombo with a large group for the Golden Jubilee Convention at Adyar. Everyone already knew of Nitya's death, and the mood was sombre. Yet Leadbeater greeted K with a strange remark, "Well, at least you are an Arhat." K said nothing.

Crowds gathered at every station as they travelled to Madras. People offered garlands and bowed before him. K remained gentle and attentive, especially toward those who were grieving Nitya, often more concerned for others than for himself.

Behind the scenes, tensions grew. Leadbeater privately rejected the spiritual 'advancements' announced at Huizen, believing none of them were true. Yet the George–Wedgwood group continued proclaiming new

Initiations. A silent divide formed within the movement, though no one wished to openly challenge Annie Besant.

K stayed apart from both sides. Out of love and respect for Annie Besant, he did not openly oppose her. He agreed to take part in ceremonies against his nature, becoming a Co-Mason and performing a Hindu ritual, only to spare her pain.

At last, Annie Besant brought everyone together and asked K directly whether he would accept them as his disciples. He replied quietly that he would take none, except perhaps her alone.

It was the closest he ever came to acknowledging a disciple.

But the loss of Nitya had already changed him. The promises he had trusted had failed. The last of his belief had already fallen away.

What remained was clarity. In that clarity, he saw that truth cannot be given by another, nor can it depend on any guru.

Did the World Teacher Speak?

The Jubilee Convention at Adyar drew large crowds and great attention. Reporters came from India and abroad. Nearly three thousand people gathered, hoping to witness something extraordinary. Rain fell steadily. As no hall was large enough, the meetings took place outdoors beneath a vast banyan tree. Loudspeakers were used for the first time.

The first day of the Convention passed quietly, and many felt a little disappointed.

The next morning, on 28 December, the Star Congress began. It was a sacred day for many. Years earlier, on this same day in 1911, K had handed out Star certificates at Varanasi, and people had fallen at his feet. Now, beneath the banyan tree, he spoke calmly about the World Teacher. He spoke of compassion, longing, and the human search for happiness.

Near the end, he said softly, "He comes only to those who want, who desire, who long..."

Then something unexpected happened.

His voice suddenly changed. It became deeper, fuller, and strangely powerful. Though the amplifiers were not yet switched on, his words rang out clearly across the gathering.

"I come for those who want sympathy, who want happiness, who are longing to be released. I come to reform and not to tear down. I come not to destroy but to build."

A hush fell over the crowd. Many felt a shiver of awe. Those close to the platform believed this was not K speaking, but Lord Maitreya using his voice. Others, including George, would later say it was simply a moment of deep inspiration and nothing more.

At the closing meeting, Annie Besant spoke with great conviction. She declared that the chosen vehicle of the World Teacher had finally been accepted. Doubt and opposition, she said, had always followed great spiritual moments.

K himself showed no uncertainty. Later, speaking to Star representatives, he urged them to guard the memory of that morning like a precious jewel. When He came again, he said, it would be an even nobler moment.

A week later, K described how he felt inside. He said it was as if a great storm had passed through him, clearing fear and confusion. He felt empty, yet pure, like a crystal vessel ready to hold something beautiful. He told Lady Emily that he felt like an empty shell, but a precious one, and believed the Lord would return whenever the world needed him.

Even Leadbeater believed that something extraordinary had taken place.

Yet doubts soon spread. Some dismissed the event. Others pointed out that no true Messiah had ever been prepared from childhood to believe himself to be one.

So the question remained. Had a divine voice spoken? Or had belief itself simply found its moment?

Voice by the Fire

After Nitya's death, Rajagopal quietly took over many of the duties Nitya had once handled. He became the Organising Secretary of the Star. He was efficient, orderly, and tireless. K valued this greatly. It was a relief to have someone dependable beside him.

Yet Rajagopal was very different from Nitya. Beneath his gentle manner lay a strong need to control. Slowly he began acting as a gatekeeper around K. He typed letters in K's name, answered messages for him, and asked people to reply privately to him instead. Those close to K noticed the difference in tone. They could tell the words were not his. Still, no one openly objected.

In May 1926, K travelled to Castle Eerde in Holland to prepare for the Star Camp at Ommen. By now he was widely recognised. On the ship, strangers stared at him and whispered his name. Even without speaking, his presence drew attention.

That summer the Star Camp at Ommen was larger than ever. Thousands arrived from many countries. Hundreds of tents covered the fields. Each evening great bonfires were lit. People sang, talked, and waited, hoping something special might happen.

K stayed at Castle Eerde and came down to the campfires dressed in flowing Indian clothes. Watching him chant by the fire many felt they were witnessing something ancient and beautiful.

He spoke several times during the camp. But one evening stood apart.

As K stood before the fire, his voice deepened. His words became strong and direct, yet full of tenderness. He spoke of truth, not as belief or authority, but as something alive and present. He urged people not to follow him, not to label him, but to look for themselves.

As he spoke, a deep stillness spread. No one moved. His face seemed changed, quiet, radiant, almost unfamiliar. Even the crackling fire seemed to soften.

When he finished, the silence remained.

Some felt certain that the World Teacher had spoken through him. Others felt it was simply the power of a human being speaking from the deepest truth he knew.

Later an old friend told K that his whole expression had changed. She said she had not seen him at all, but it seemed as though someone else was speaking through him.

K listened gently and smiled. He said only that he wished he could have seen it too.

Once again, the question lingered in the night air.

Was it a divine voice? Or the awakening of something far simpler, far closer, and deeply human?

Dark Doubts

The camp was filled with excitement. Many people felt uplifted and blessed. Annie Besant herself seemed deeply moved. But while they sat together, Wedgwood leaned toward her and whispered something that instantly troubled her.

After the meeting, Annie Besant asked Rajagopal to take K back to the Castle. A little later she went to his room. What she said there shocked him deeply. She told him, quite seriously, that a powerful black magician she knew had spoken through him.

K was stunned. It hurt him deeply to hear such words from Amma, whom he loved and trusted more than anyone else. If she truly believed this, he said quietly, he would never speak in public again.

The moment distressed Annie Besant. She never again accused him of being influenced by dark forces. Yet the harm had already been done. From then on, Wedgwood repeated the idea of a 'black magician' whenever he wished to create doubt or confusion about K.

Soon the camp split into two groups. Some were certain that Lord Maitreya had spoken. They felt a tender, powerful presence and trusted it fully. Others, influenced by Wedgwood, began to whisper and argue. Rumours spread quickly.

On the final evening of the camp, K spoke again. Troubled by all the talk, he spoke straight from his heart. His closing words stunned everyone.

"You may take my heart and eat it, you may take my blood and drink it, and I shall not mind, because I have so much and you have so little."

Annie Besant was now deeply torn. Confused and unhappy, she even thought of resigning as President of the Theosophical Society. She wrote to Leadbeater, who firmly advised her not to step down.

She felt caught between two worlds. On one side was her love for K. On the other side were her lifelong beliefs, her faith in the Masters, and her sense of duty.

At last she chose a middle path. Instead of returning to India, she decided to travel with K to America and speak about the coming World Teacher. It was her way of standing by him, without fully letting go of the beliefs she still held.

So the quiet division continued to grow.

A Brother's Grief

K returned briefly to London after the Ommen Camp. Soon after, he sailed to America with Annie Besant, Rajagopal, and Rosalind. Annie Besant planned a large lecture tour, speaking everywhere about the coming World Teacher.

Their arrival in New York created both excitement and trouble. Rumours had spread that a Messiah was arriving. Reporters rushed onto the ship, expecting something grand. Instead, they found a shy young man dressed simply in Western clothes.

Some newspapers mocked him. One headline called him a 'Messiah in tennis flannels'. A few reporters were kind, but many were cruel. K answered their questions calmly, but the attention embarrassed him deeply.

Soon the press turned to his personal life. They noticed Rosalind often beside him and asked blunt questions about marriage. K replied simply that people marry because they feel lonely, and that he had never known loneliness. The rumours only increased, leaving him feeling exposed and uncomfortable.

After a disappointing convention in Chicago, K travelled briefly to Virginia and then on to Ojai. It was his first return since his brother Nitya's death.

The moment he entered Arya Vihara, memories overwhelmed him. The hills, the rooms, the silence, everything reminded him of Nitya. For a moment K felt as if he could almost see him again and even sense him nearby. Later he wrote that when he stepped into the room where his brother had been ill, his body suddenly broke down and wept, even though inwardly he felt calm.

It was a strange experience for him.

In the quiet room, he felt Nitya's presence strongly. It seemed almost physical, as though he might see him or even reach out and touch him. "I wasn't really upset", he wrote later, "but my body was in an extraordinary state. My body cried".

They had lived together there, suffered together during illness, and shared many quiet happy hours. Looking around at the familiar walls and the sunlight falling through the windows, K realised he would now have to learn, slowly and painfully, to live without his brother's physical presence.

Yet something remarkable took place. K did not cling to his grief, nor did he push it away. The pain softened on its own. The sharp edge of sorrow slowly faded, leaving behind a quiet, tender affection.

So he moved forward, not hardened by loss, but deepened by it. He learned to live with life as it is, moment by moment, without being held by the past.

Love is Never Possessive

K developed a painful swelling in his right chest and consulted a doctor in Hollywood. The doctors assured him it was not serious, but he advised him not to travel. This meant he could not return to India for the Theosophical Convention at Varanasi, which deeply disappointed Annie Besant.

Lady Emily and her daughter Mary were asked to come to Ojai to help care for him. They both came gladly. Their visit became the longest time they had ever spent continuously with K.

They lived close together. K, Annie Besant, and Rajagopal stayed at Arya Vihara. Lady Emily and Mary lived nearby. They shared all their meals, and the days took on a warm, family-like feeling.

K enjoyed the quiet weeks in Ojai. In the evenings, he went on long walks, watching the sun sink behind the hills. He began writing gentle poems inspired by the fading light.

The Process continued, but more mildly. At times, sharp pain would seize him, and he would briefly lose awareness. Mary cared for him patiently. During these moments, he would speak like a child, calling her his mother and trusting in her kindness.

In the mornings, K was cheerful and playful. He taught Mary to drive the new car, though his quick impatience sometimes made her feel nervous. Once, she drove off alone, but could not manage to reverse the car. K waited anxiously until she finally returned on foot, tired, but safe.

During these weeks, K was unusually open and human. Lady Emily's affection for him slowly deepened into strong attachment. K noticed this and spoke to her gently, but with clarity. He told her that love is beautiful when it is free, but the moment it becomes possessive, it loses its purity.

"We all love one another", he said, "and that is enough. But if I become necessary to you, it spoils that love."

Then he added softly, "Everyone seems to think they have some special claim on me".

In this quiet moment, there was a lesson K lived by. Love does not bind, own, or demand. True love sets free.

When Authority Fades

Annie Besant remained deeply involved in her Theosophical work at Ojai. She loved the valley and bought more than 450 acres of land near Arya Vihara. She dreamed of building a school and a centre for the World Teacher. To support this vision, she formed the Happy Valley Foundation and raised large sums of money. The land was secured, but the school itself would come into being only many years later, long after her lifetime.

During these months, Annie Besant felt closer to K than ever before. Slowly, her belief changed. She no longer felt that the World Teacher spoke through him only at special moments. She now believed that K's own consciousness had fully merged with Lord Maitreya.

K himself felt that something important was unfolding. In a letter, he wrote that his 'cup was nearly full' and that he longed to bring happiness to all.

Before leaving Ojai, Annie Besant made a bold statement to the American press. She declared that the Divine Spirit had descended upon him and announced firmly, "The World Teacher is here".

The news spread quickly across the world.

Yet soon after, something quiet yet decisive began to change.

In Paris, K spoke to a small group and referred to the Masters as 'incidents'. For devoted Theosophists, especially members of the Esoteric Section, whose faith rested on the Masters, this was deeply unsettling. If the World Teacher spoke this way, what were they now to believe?

Before the Ommen Camp, while staying at Castle Eerde, K fell ill with severe bronchitis and was confined to bed. Friends gathered around him and fussed over his care, each wanting to help in their own way. Even then, he remained calm and quietly amused by their anxious attention. When he recovered enough to speak, his words carried a new clarity and strength.

He spoke of liberation.

No Master, guru, or authority, he said, could lead another person to liberation. Liberation could not be given; it had to be discovered. No one should depend on him. If he became necessary to them, they would be lost when he was gone. Each person had to look within and find out for themselves.

These words disturbed many. For those trained to rely on spiritual authority, they felt it was frightening. But K was unmoved. Belief, hierarchy, and dependence no longer held meaning for him.

Around this time, another quiet struggle was taking place inside him.

For a short while, K felt a strong wish to renounce the world. He wanted to become a sanyasi, a monk in India who gives up family, comfort, and possessions, and wears a simple yellow robe. He even wrote that he had 'mentally and emotionally put on the yellow robe'. He felt like shouting from the mountaintop. He wanted to give up everything and live only for truth.

To many people, this might sound noble and beautiful. And it was sincere.

But K looked at it very carefully.

He saw something surprising. The wish to renounce was still a wish. It was still a desire. Even the desire to be free from desire was, in fact, another form of desire.

If he ran away from the world, would that truly bring freedom? Or was it just another escape?

He did not become a monk. He did not put on the yellow robe. He did not choose a special outer life.

Instead, he chose something far more difficult. To live in the world inwardly without belonging to it.

He saw clearly that freedom was not in changing clothes, names, or places. It was in understanding oneself completely.

Without protest or rebellion, authority was loosening its hold, not only outer authority, but the subtle authority of his own desires.

Quietly, without announcements or banners, something freer and truer began to take its place.

I Am the Teacher

For many years, members of the Star waited for the coming of a great World Teacher. They believed that a divine teacher would appear to guide humanity.

When K began to speak with unusual power, many listeners felt something extraordinary. His voice was calm yet compelling. People sat in deep silence. Some believed they were hearing the voice of Lord Maitreya through him. Slowly the feeling spread through the crowds. Many began to believe the long-awaited moment had arrived. The Teacher was no longer speaking through K. The Teacher was speaking as K.

Yet K himself never publicly claimed to be the World Teacher. He even told Annie Besant that he disliked people speaking of him in that way.

In the meantime, the leaders of the Star began reshaping the organisation. Lady Emily and Rajagopal rewrote its aims to serve the World Teacher, now believed to be present. Rajagopal became the Chief Organiser. K watched quietly. These changes did not interest him much.

When Raja arrived from India, he was deeply troubled. As a devoted Theosophist he believed firmly that the World Teacher and the human 'vehicle' could never be the same. To him, K could only be someone through whom the Teacher might sometimes speak.

One morning, instead of giving a talk, K read poetry. A discussion followed. Raja objected strongly to calling K the World Teacher. Others disagreed, and the atmosphere grew tense.

Later K took Raja for a long walk and spoke openly. Without hesitation, he said he now knew clearly that he was the Teacher. The moment was quiet and private, not a public declaration. At that time K was still speaking within the language of the Theosophical movement, ideas he would later leave behind.

To K, this was not a claim or a declaration. It was something he felt with complete certainty within himself. In his own words, he had reached his goal. To him, the Teacher was no longer something outside. It was what he had become.

Raja listened calmly and appeared to accept what K said. But inwardly he remained unconvinced. To him, K seemed to be speaking from personality, not from spiritual authority.

K then wrote to Annie Besant, addressing her as 'Mother', as he always did. He said the fulfilment of many lives had come. Raja carried the note to her. What passed between them is not known. However, when Raja returned, he spoke firmly to the group. He said that K was not the Lord. His words sounded cold and distant, and moved no one. K was not present during this talk.

The next morning K spoke again, as if he had known of Raja's talk. He spoke quietly of a long journey of struggle, sorrow, and patience. He spoke of reaching a mountain peak and entering the flame of truth. After that, he said, nothing else mattered. His words touched many hearts, unlike Raja's cold lecture.

The gathering sat in deep silence. Many felt something profound had been said, and Raja could say nothing more.

Seeing Beyond the Masters

In early August, the group moved from Castle Eerde to Ommen for the great Star Camp. Nearly three thousand people gathered there from many lands, cultures, and beliefs, more than ever before in one place. Some slept in tents, others in nearby towns. One young man even walked for weeks just to attend. When people collected money for his return, he chose instead to stay and later helped care for the camp.

The evenings were the heart of Ommen.

At sunset, a great fire was lit. Flames rose into the darkening sky, lighting thousands of silent faces. K would stand quietly before the fire and then speak or chant. His voice moved gently across the crowd. Many felt a deep stillness, as if words and silence had become one.

Yet beneath the beauty, confusion was growing.

Many were troubled by what K had recently said about Masters and authority. They had spent years believing in a hidden hierarchy that guided humanity. Now they wondered what was real.

On 2 August, K spoke directly to this confusion.

He told them that as a child he had seen Krishna, just as his mother believed. Later, through the Theosophists, he had seen the Masters as they were described to him. Then he had seen Lord Maitreya. Still later, the Buddha. Each vision had felt real until he saw something deeper beyond them.

He explained that what he called the Beloved was not a single person or form. To him, it was everything. The sky, a flower, a suffering human being, all of life itself. Names did not matter. Forms did not matter.

He said that people had leaned too long on authority, on teachers, protectors, and explanations. Truth, he said, could never be handed down. It had to be discovered within oneself.

He was not asking anyone to believe him. He was asking them to look for themselves.

"Does it matter," he asked gently, "from which cup you drink, if the water is pure and truly quenches your thirst?"

Many were deeply moved. Others felt unsettled.

Annie Besant arrived a day later and missed this talk. K knew it might hurt her, and he would never wish that. In her absence, he spoke with a rare freedom.

Yet something had quietly shifted, and would not return to what it had been.

Truth and Theosophy

Annie Besant soon learned of K's talk on 2 August. What he had said disturbed her deeply. It sounded nothing like the voice of Lord Maitreya as she understood it. To her, it seemed to be K's own human voice, not that of the World Teacher.

This troubled her even more because, for years, she herself had urged people to keep an open mind. She had often said that when the Lord spoke, His words might be new and unexpected. Yet now, when K's words truly challenged tradition, her own certainty began to waver.

When the camp officially opened on 7 August, Annie Besant still spoke with conviction. Her theme remained the same. She said, "The World Teacher is here". The camp closed quietly on 12 August, with nothing dramatic on the surface.

After Annie Besant returned to Huizen, a smaller Service Camp was held for volunteers who had missed earlier meetings. K spoke again. This time, his words unsettled many deeply. No official notes of this talk survived. They were likely destroyed out of care for Annie Besant's feelings. One sentence, however, remained in Lady Emily's diary.

"You cannot really help until you are yourself beyond the need of help."

Those present were devoted Theosophists. To them, Theosophy itself was the Truth, not what K was now saying. Later, Peter Freedman, a General Secretary of the Theosophical Society in Wales, wrote that K openly admitted he could not understand Theosophical books or their language. None of the lectures he had heard convinced him that Truth had been found.

Lady De La Warr, a loyal Theosophist who loved K, was shaken when she heard what he had said. K wrote to her gently. He said he had not realised he had caused pain and was truly sorry. When they met later, she reassured him. She was not hurt; she simply disagreed. K felt relieved. To him, disagreement was honest. Hurt was not.

Annie Besant, however, remained deeply troubled. She now sensed a widening distance. On one side stood the Esoteric teachings she had served all her life. On the other stood K, whom she had raised and presented to the world as the coming World Teacher. Yet what he was now saying seemed to belong to neither world.

Still, she did not openly oppose him. Out of love and loyalty she continued to stand beside him, hoping that what he was saying might somehow still fit within the larger vision she had long believed in.

Most unsettling of all was that young people were gathering around him, drawn not by Theosophy's past, but by something fresh and direct in his words. To Annie Besant, it felt as though the great structure she had patiently built over many years was slowly slipping away.

Wisdom Beyond Years

After the camp, K travelled briefly to Montesano and then to Paris. There, a well-known sculptor, Antoine Bourdelle, asked him to sit for a sculpture. For eight days in September, K spent several hours each day posing quietly while the elderly artist worked with deep concentration. Bourdelle hoped to create a life-sized statue, but time allowed only a bust.

The sculptor was deeply moved by K. As he watched and listened, he seemed almost spellbound. Bourdelle said with wonder that hearing Krishnamurti speak was astonishing, so much wisdom in someone so young. He even said that if he were fifteen again, he would have followed him.

The finished bust, considered one of Bourdelle's finest works, still stands today in a museum in Paris.

K returned to London on 30 September and stayed with Lady Emily. The next evening, he dined with Annie Besant at Buckingham Street to celebrate her eightieth birthday. The occasion carried an unexpected surprise.

Mrs Percy Douglas-Hamilton, who had died recently, had left Annie Besant a remarkable gift in her will—£25,000, the largest sum she had ever received as a birthday present. The same will also set aside £10,000 for the Order of the Star.

By then Annie Besant's health had begun to weaken, and those around her felt a quiet respect for her long life of service. Those present later remembered the evening as warm and respectful, though beneath the courtesy there was also a quiet awareness that K's path was beginning to move in a new direction. The dinner seemed to mark the end of one chapter and the beginning of another.

Soon after, quiet yet important changes began to take place. Rajagopal and Rosalind were married in London. The wedding was attended by Jadu, a young Indian who had recently become a close friend and was now almost a constant companion of K, travelling with him everywhere.

The newly married Rajagopals then travelled to Ojai, where Arya Vihara became their home. K, who was away at Eerde for the Star Camp, could not attend the wedding.

Later, K joined Annie Besant at Marseilles for the journey back to India. Several friends travelled with them by ship. During the voyage, tragedy struck once more. Dr Mary Rocke, one of K's oldest and most trusted friends, slipped on the ship's stairs and died instantly.

Her sudden death saddened K deeply. Once again, life reminded him how fragile human bonds can be, and how quietly sorrow can return, even when one has learned much about living.

Not Even a Fragment

When the ship reached Bombay on 27 October, large crowds and reporters were waiting. Annie Besant spoke with her usual brilliance, praising him before the press. Yet this time, her words carried a careful change. She said that not the full World Teacher, but only a fragment of a great universal consciousness, had blended with him.

Her speech was grand and moving. She spoke of K as chosen and worthy, now returned to his own people, yet belonging to the whole world. Many listeners were deeply moved. Some almost began to worship him.

Among Theosophists, however, her statement caused confusion.

George Arundale reacted sharply. He wrote that he believed not even a fragment of the Lord's consciousness was present in K. His words were polite, but his disbelief was clear.

Leadbeater, writing from Sydney, was more careful. In a birthday message to Annie Besant, he praised her for 'training and caring for the vehicle of the World Teacher,' comparing K to a flower she had nurtured. The words sounded admiring, yet many sensed a quiet distance beneath them.

By now, Leadbeater had fallen out with George and Wedgwood, but he remained friendly toward K. When K met him at Adyar, they went for a long walk. K spoke openly about his doubts and inner struggles. Leadbeater listened without arguing. This made K feel, perhaps wrongly, that he agreed with him.

In public, both Annie Besant and Leadbeater continued to support K. This only increased the questions people asked him. Again and again, he was asked whether he was the Christ. The question embarrassed him deeply.

After the convention, the first Star Camp in India was held near Adyar. K spoke twice and answered questions for hours. He then travelled across India, addressing large audiences. The strain was heavy.

With Rajagopal now married, Jadu travelled with K instead. Gentle, devoted, and without any wish to control, he soon became K's close attendant and companion, part of the small circle that now gathered around him.

Still weak from illness, K pushed himself on. By February 1928 he was completely exhausted and left India for Europe. Jadu travelled beside him. K carried with him no certainty, only questions about truth, authority, and belief. Those questions would soon lead him to challenge the very ideas that had once shaped his life.

A Quiet Turning

K's journey to Europe began quietly, on a slow ship to Genoa. For the first time, fellow passengers asked him to speak, and he agreed. After Genoa, he travelled through

France, Ommen, and finally London. On 31 March, he gave his first public talk in England. The halls overflowed. Many who came were not Theosophists and had never heard of the Star. They came simply to listen.

Soon after, K sailed to America and travelled on to Ojai for rest. Rosalind and Rajagopal, now married, welcomed him warmly. He was happy to see the young trees he had planted earlier now growing strong.

On 15 May, K spoke at the Hollywood Bowl. Nearly 16,000 people sat in complete silence, listening to his talk on *Happiness through Liberation*. Most had no interest in the idea of a World Teacher. They listened because his words spoke directly to their lives.

At the same time, Annie Besant introduced a new idea called the World Mother, identified with the Virgin Mary. She declared that Rukmini Arundale was her chosen vehicle. The announcement caused confusion and drew press attention. Journalists now questioned K not only about the World Teacher but also about the World Mother. Spiritual authority seemed to multiply, and many no longer knew whom to trust.

A Star Camp followed in Ojai, held on land Annie Besant had bought for the future. About a thousand people attended. Morning talks were open to all and held beneath ancient oak trees, later called the Oak Grove. Many who came were neither Theosophists nor Star members. Yet they returned each morning, drawn by the simplicity of K's words.

Helen, an old friend, also attended. Their affection remained gentle and unchanged.

After the camp, K returned to Europe. In Paris, he spoke to a packed hall. Later, he gave a radio talk on happiness from the Eiffel Tower, reaching nearly two million listeners.

By now, K was unwell with bronchitis. From his bed, he wrote kindly to Annie Besant, knowing that his recent words had troubled her. Though she disagreed deeply with him, her love did not fade. Soon her health collapsed, and cruel rumours blamed K for it.

K rejected such ideas. He neither defended himself nor blamed anyone. Something within him was turning quietly away from crowds, titles, and authority toward a truth that asked for no followers at all.

I Am Not Divine

K spoke more openly than ever before at the Ommen Camp.

Annie Besant was not present. Without the fear of hurting her, K spoke to the National Organisers of the Order of the Star with complete honesty. He warned them that if the Order ever claimed to own Truth, he would dissolve it at once. Truth, he said, could never belong to any organisation.

In meetings at Eerde, he explained what he meant by the term World Teacher. There existed, he said, a living intelligence without beginning or end, which was the source of all life. The Buddha and the Christ had touched this intelligence. Anyone who lived with deep awareness could touch Truth. This Life had no form and belonged to everyone.

Again and again, he urged people to trust their own understanding. He asked them not to depend on interpreters or spiritual authorities. Even long-held beliefs, he warned, would soon be shaken.

Questions poured in. Did he want disciples? What about rituals? Why deny stages on the spiritual path? Was he the Christ returned?

K answered calmly and firmly.

He wanted no disciples. Truth could not be found by following a person. Worship of personalities only created confusion. Rituals were unnecessary for inner freedom. Liberation, he said, could happen instantly, not after climbing spiritual ladders.

He refused to be treated as an authority. He warned people not to lean on him. Truth, he said, was like fresh mountain air; once trapped, it lost its life.

He explained that he had never denied God. What he rejected were fear-filled ideas attached to the word.

He preferred to speak of Life, alive in every human being. When fear ended, strict morality faded, and love for life took its place.

When asked directly whether he was the Christ, K replied in a way that unsettled many. If he said yes, people would turn him into an authority. If he said no, they would do the same. Truth, he said, had nothing to do with who he was. People cared more about the container than what it held.

He ended the camp with a reminder. Thousands had attended these meetings. If even a few truly understood, the world could change, not slowly, but at once.

Many long-standing Theosophists were confused. This was not the World Teacher they had imagined. Even Lady Emily admitted her uncertainty. After years of waiting, people felt hurt when he asked them to think for themselves. Some returned home shaken.

Yet beneath the confusion, authority was fading, and inner responsibility was awakening.

A Door Is Closed

After the Ommen Camp, K went to St Moritz in Switzerland to rest. Raja soon joined him there. Lady Emily, Mary, Rajagopal, and Jadu were also with them. They stayed in a quiet chalet overlooking Lake Silvaplana.

During this peaceful break, K and Raja spent long hours talking alone. No one knows exactly what was said. But Raja was very close to Annie Besant, and it is likely he later shared these conversations with her.

From Switzerland, K travelled to Paris. He then returned to Eerde and sailed with Jadu for Colombo.

During the journey, Raja wrote to him. In the letter he explained that Annie Besant and Leadbeater were unhappy. K would not support ideas they deeply valued, such as the Liberal Catholic Church, Freemasonry, or the idea of the World Mother.

When the ship reached Aden, K wrote honestly to Lady Emily. He said there was a direct way to Truth and that everything else was a distraction.

He saw clearly that Raja had never fully agreed with him. Since he would not change his position, he felt Annie Besant and Leadbeater would have to rethink the Esoteric Section of the Theosophical Society. He even hinted he might take some 'direct action'. He never explained what this action might be, and later it seemed to pass from his mind.

K arrived in Colombo on 5 November and went on to Adyar. Annie Besant was still in Delhi. Soon, however, he received a letter from her that stunned him.

She wrote that she was suspending the Esoteric Section indefinitely. She placed all teaching responsibility in K's hands, calling him 'the only authority'.

This came as a complete surprise to K. It was unlike Annie Besant, and he had not expected such a step from her. It seemed, in a quiet way, to echo his earlier thought of 'direct action', though he himself had done nothing. Deeply moved, he wrote to Lady Emily, praising Annie Besant's courage. To build something over a lifetime and then set it aside for something greater, he said, was the noblest act a human being could perform.

The Esoteric Section had been founded in 1889 and was seen as the heart of the Society. Many believed it to be the gateway to higher wisdom. By closing it, Annie Besant had shaken the entire movement.

Some people felt relieved. Others were angry. Thousands had not been asked for their opinion.

If the Esoteric Section mattered deeply to anyone, it was Annie Besant above all. Her decision showed both her trust in K and her rare courage. She knew there would be criticism and accepted it quietly.

Later, George Arundale spoke to K in private. His words were calm and final. "You go your way," he said. "And we will go ours."

The door was now closed.

The Natural Flower

The Process returned once more. This time it troubled K deeply.

He suffered intense pain in his head and spine. The pain left him weak and exhausted. After giving a few talks, he was forced to rest through the winter.

Some people around him felt confused. Mary especially sensed that many believed K was divine and expected everyone else to become like him. This idea disturbed her. If everyone became the same, she felt, the world would lose its movement and come to a halt.

K sensed her unease. On Lady Emily's birthday he wrote a gentle message meant especially for Mary, hoping to clear the misunderstanding. He said that he was not divine. He was, he wrote, "the natural flower of the world."

Perfection, he explained, was not something strange or abnormal. If all human beings lived with the same clarity and freedom, life would become more beautiful, not frozen or lifeless.

Around the same time he wrote firmly to Raja. He said he would follow only the path he knew to be true. Truth, he wrote, was vast, like the open sky. People argued endlessly over passing clouds, forgetting the sky itself.

Meanwhile a long-held dream began to take shape.

Land was acquired at Rajghat in Varanasi along the banks of the Ganges. An ancient path, known as the Pilgrim's Path, believed to have been walked by the Buddha after his first sermon at Sarnath, passed through this land. For centuries it had carried the footsteps of seekers moving between Sarnath and Kashi. On this quiet ground the Rajghat School would later be built, a place for learning, simplicity, and freedom. In time a women's college also grew beside it.

Soon after, the Theosophical Society Convention was held in Varanasi. With Annie Besant and Leadbeater absent, K presided alone. Annie Besant had instructed that no ceremonies be held inside the compound, and her wish was followed carefully.

Yet just outside the grounds, George held church services attended by many members. The contrast was clear.

Annie Besant tried to hold two worlds together. She quoted the Bhagavad Gita, saying that people reach truth by many paths. In *The Theosophist* she wrote that K urged people to abandon all forms, but quietly added that this did not apply to her. She believed his teaching was meant mainly for others, not for long-established leaders like herself. Her effort to balance authority with freedom only increased the confusion.

K's message, however, was simple and firm. Truth does not belong to any form. It cannot be owned by a leader or protected by an organisation. It must be lived, not guarded. And like a flower, it must grow naturally.

Truth Is a Pathless Land

It was the morning of 3 August 1929 at the Star Camp at Ommen. Annie Besant sat in the front rows. Nearly three thousand members of the Order of the Star gathered beneath the tall beech trees. Something extraordinary was about to unfold.

Hundreds of tents from the Star Camp stretched across the fields like a small temporary village. Thousands more were listening on the radio across Europe. Many had waited eighteen years for this moment, when the World Teacher would finally speak and lead them. The great crowd waited in deep, expectant silence.

K rose and calmly announced that he was dissolving the Order of the Star, the very organisation created to prepare the world for him.

For a moment the gathering did not quite understand what they had heard.

There was no anger in his voice. No drama. He explained quietly that the decision had not been sudden. For nearly two years he had thought about it deeply. Truth, he said, was far too alive to be locked inside any organisation.

Then he spoke the words that would echo around the world.

"Truth is a pathless land."

For several moments the vast gathering remained silent. The sentence was simple, yet shook the whole movement.

What he meant was both simple and demanding. There is no ready-made path to truth. No guru who can walk ahead of you. No authority who can think on your behalf. Each human being must discover it directly through their own understanding.

With those quiet words, K stepped away from the role the world had prepared for him, leaving each person to find out for themselves.

Truth, he said, cannot be reached by following a religion, a leader, a book, or a group. It cannot be organised.

The moment people build a path to it, put up signs, and tell others to follow, truth becomes small, fixed, and lifeless.

Belief, he explained, is personal. But when belief becomes organised it turns into rules, and when rules harden they become prisons.

He warned that spiritual organisations often become crutches. Instead of strengthening the human mind, they weaken it. Instead of helping people discover truth, they encourage dependence.

That is why, he said, he did not want followers. The moment you follow a person, you stop following truth.

He made it clear that he was not starting a new religion or a new philosophy. He had only one concern, to help human beings become free, free from fear, authority, and from the need to be guided.

People often asked why he travelled and spoke if he did not want followers. His answer was quiet and firm. Even if one person truly listened and became inwardly free, that was enough.

Numbers meant nothing to him. Thousands repeating words without understanding were useless. A few who truly saw were everything.

For eighteen years, he reminded them, people had waited for a Teacher who would lift them, protect them, and save them. Now he asked a difficult question.

Had this belief made them freer? Or had it only given them comfort and identity?

Freedom, he said, cannot be given from outside. No ritual, ceremony, sacrifice, or organisation can deliver it. Even devotion becomes a chain if it replaces understanding.

The key to freedom lies within each person. No one holds it for you. No one can open the door on your behalf. There was no path laid out before them and no guru to follow.

There was only the responsibility and beauty of seeing for oneself.

No path. No guru. Just you.

He ended by saying that those who truly wished to understand would walk together, not because of belief or authority, but because of friendship and shared clarity. Such people, he said, would challenge false values, empty traditions, and lifeless ideas.

That, he said, was his purpose.

When he finished speaking, the Order of the Star no longer existed.

For Annie Besant, the moment was heartbreaking. Decades of work, hope, and sacrifice seemed to collapse in a single morning. She had built the Order to present the World Teacher to the world, and now the Teacher himself had set it aside.

Yet she did not protest.

Annie Besant had always loved truth more than comfort. She had often warned against turning living ideas into rigid beliefs. Now she recognised that K had done exactly what truth demanded, even though it broke her heart.

After the dissolution, K stepped away from all organisations. Camps were opened to everyone. Properties were returned. Structures quietly disappeared.

Many Theosophists were shaken and angry. They wanted paths, teachers, and certainty. A pathless land frightened them. Within weeks pressure grew, and Annie Besant reopened the Esoteric Section so members could follow the paths they felt they needed.

But her devotion to K never faded. She understood, at last, that he was not pointing to himself but to freedom. And freedom, she knew, could never be organised or controlled.

Leaving the Old Path

By the end of 1929, it had become clear that the path prepared for him could no longer continue.

Ideas had broken apart. Expectations no longer matched reality. The paths were beginning to separate.

Yet his step was not a rejection of Annie Besant herself, whom he continued to respect and love deeply.

Some leaders spoke openly of their disappointment. Others quietly withdrew.

When he returned to Adyar for the December convention, much had changed. The long walks and deep conversations he once shared with close companions were gone.

The authority that had once surrounded him no longer felt real, either to him or to others.

K himself understood this clearly. He was no longer the fragile boy discovered on the Adyar beach. He had grown into something new that the old system could not hold.

During the convention, K confided to Lady Emily that he wanted to leave it all behind. He felt trapped in ceremonies, spiritual games, and struggles for authority. Annie Besant still spoke of him as the World Teacher while holding on to rituals he had firmly rejected. This saddened him deeply. He felt that people were being treated like children, and so they remained children.

In 1930, the break became final. K formally resigned from the Theosophical Society, just a year after dissolving the Order of the Star.

Yet Annie Besant's love for him did not fade. She still believed he was the World Teacher, even though she could not understand why the Masters no longer mattered to him. When he spoke, she no longer sat on the platform. Instead, she sat quietly among the listeners, a small but touching sign of humility.

Many years later, K spoke of her with tenderness.

He said softly that if Amma had been younger, she would have understood.

For Annie Besant, the loss was painful. The work that had guided her life fell away in her final years. Lady Emily also felt lost. She had built her life around the Order of the Star. When it ended, her sense of purpose disappeared. A few years later, she too resigned from the Society.

For younger followers, the shock was even greater. Many had left families and careers, believing they were following a divine plan. Now that plan had vanished. The ground beneath them seemed to disappear. Confusion and sadness followed.

K, however, did not look back. He simply moved forward.

Between 1930 and 1931, he travelled widely across Europe. He spoke against nationalism and organised religion. In one city, angry extremists threatened his life, and police guarded him throughout his stay. Often he returned to Ojai to rest and then set out again to speak.

In August 1931, another sorrow struck. Jadu, now his close and constant companion, died suddenly at the age of thirty-five. Jadu had much of the same sweetness K had once known in Nitya. There was in him a natural gentleness, free of any need to dominate or control. K was deeply shaken. Exhausted and unwell, he returned to Ojai to recover. He stayed with the Rajagopals and grew fond of their baby daughter, Radha.

Periods of solitude became precious to him. Alone in the house, he cooked for himself, walked in nature, watched his thoughts, and sat quietly. He once wrote that he observed thought "like a cat watching a mouse." When a reporter asked if he was the Christ, he replied gently, "Yes—in a true sense—but not in the usual way."

In those quiet years, a new clarity was unfolding in him. He was no longer trying to become something. Instead, he was learning to observe life exactly as it was, without authority, belief, or tradition to stand in the way.

Lady Emily found this time the hardest. Without Theosophy, K's words felt distant to her. Sensing her pain, he wrote long letters. He tried to explain that clarity was not an escape from life, but a deeper meeting with it. It was not running away from sorrow or fear, but understanding them fully.

He wrote that he was trying to build a bridge for others, not away from life, but to live more fully. Still, he admitted that truth could never be fully put into words. What was spoken was never the thing itself.

Something had changed in him.

Around this time, K almost completely lost his memory of the past. A deep quietness came over him. The identity formed by Theosophy, titles, and roles had quietly faded away. What remained was freshness, untouched by belief or history. It was as though the past had fallen away from him, like an empty shell.

At times, when people reminded him of earlier events in his life, they seemed to him almost like stories about someone else.

Once, while speaking of this, he said he could not even remember Nitya's face, though he had loved his brother deeply all his life. Then he added quietly, almost mysteriously, "Of course I can, if I really want to."

The old path had ended. A new life had begun, without ready-made paths or guides to follow. There was no doctrine, no Master, no fixed path to follow.

From this point onward, his message would remain the same for the rest of his life. Truth, he said, cannot be organised, taught, or handed down. It must be discovered freshly by each human being.

And so began the journey he would later describe in simple words. Truth is a pathless land.

Passing On

One by one, those close to him left. First Nitya, then Dr Rocke. Now it was Jadu.

The circle around him was growing smaller.

Around him now gathered a younger group of helpers. They were not shaped by Theosophical authority. They were drawn instead to a new way of living that K spoke about, a life without fear, belief, or dependence.

Annie Besant, once the powerful presence of his youth, was now growing weak. When K visited her in December 1932, she was losing her memory but could still recognise him. She spoke lovingly of how she had raised him and his brother. But her memory was fading. She repeated the same stories again and again, living more in the past than in the present. On 20 September 1933, she died peacefully at Adyar.

Annie Besant had been an extraordinary woman. She played an important role in India's freedom movement. But for K, her greatest role was personal. She had protected him and Nitya as her own children. She had educated them. She had given her life to what she believed was a great spiritual mission centred on him.

Even after K walked away from Theosophy, he never walked away from her. He loved her deeply and respected her above all others.

Soon after her death, K was invited to speak at the closing of the Theosophical Convention. Someone asked what tribute he would offer to the woman who had guided and protected him. K replied simply. He said she had been their mother who had cared for them. And the greatest thing she had done, he added, was never telling him what to think or what to do. She had left him free. That, he said, was the highest tribute he could give her.

With Annie Besant's passing, K's last emotional bond with the Theosophical Society dissolved. He now went fully his own way. Krishnamurti Foundations gradually arose in different countries. They were not organisations of belief or membership. Their purpose was simply to preserve his teachings, organise his talks, and support the schools he cared about.

Barely six months later, on 1 March 1934, Leadbeater died in Australia. K was in Sydney at the time and attended his cremation. Writing later to a close friend, he noted how many people felt lost. They wondered who would now tell them how far they had progressed spiritually. This need for authority, for someone to reassure them, was exactly what K had always questioned.

With the deaths of Annie Besant and Leadbeater, a whole chapter of Theosophical history came to an end. Others followed over time, former leaders, devoted supporters, once famous figures, each fading quietly into the past.

Lady Emily lived for many more years. But after the 1930s she could no longer truly understand K's talks. Still, her affection never faded. In her old age, when memory itself slipped away, K would sit beside her whenever he visited London. He held her hand and softly chanted. She did not know the meaning of the chant, but it filled her with comfort and joy.

K himself moved forward, unchanged in his commitment to truth. He travelled widely, spoke tirelessly, and lived simply. He did not replace old beliefs with new ones, and he did not gather followers.

In his family life, K had long lived apart. After Nitya's death he had little contact with his blood relatives. His father had died early. His elder brother Sivaram, deeply religious and rooted in tradition, had been distant for many years. They met only once, in 1947.

During that meeting Sivaram asked him what the self was. K replied quietly that the self was nothing more than a collection of memories. Sivaram could not accept this. The conversation ended there. Sivaram died a few years later.

Yet K did not forget family responsibility. During that meeting he had promised to care for Sivaram's children, and he kept that promise faithfully. He supported their education and guided their work.

One nephew, Narayan, became especially close to him and later devoted his life to education at Rishi Valley School. K followed his work with great interest and helped whenever needed.

Though K did not believe that blood relationships were spiritually special, he believed deeply in care, responsibility, and affection.

Near the end of his life, during his final visit to Ojai in February 1986, he quietly gave away many of his personal belongings to another nephew. There was no ceremony and no display of emotion. It was a simple passing on, as though gently setting the past aside.

By then almost everyone who had shaped his early life had become history. Guardians, friends, movements, beliefs, all had fallen away, like scaffolding removed once a building is complete.

What remained was a man inwardly free. Untouched by memory. Unbound by tradition.

From that stillness came a voice that did not belong to the past, the voice of a teacher who asked nothing of others except that they look, listen, and discover truth for themselves.

A Life Without Anchors

K was no longer becoming something. He had become. Not through effort. Not through time. It was as if a door had closed behind him and the past could no longer follow. What had happened within him was not growth. It was flowering.

This inward ending was so complete that memory itself seemed to loosen its hold. The mind no longer lived in the images and experiences it had gathered. The past had fallen away, leaving a strange freshness in which each moment stood alone.

Outwardly, little had change. He remained simple. Curious. Light in manner. He laughed easily. His curiosity remained alive, even about technology. In later years, he questioned scientists about computers and artificial intelligence. There was no pose of holiness about him.

But inwardly there was a vast stillness. His mind was empty. Not blank. Not passive. But alert. Fresh. Each moment seemed untouched by the one before. People often felt that he understood a question before it was fully asked. His replies came without hesitation. Clear.

He had become a teacher, but not the teacher people once imagined. He did not stand above others. He stood with them. He asked for no loyalty. He accepted no disciples.

If people tried to follow him, he gently turned them back to themselves.

He was often alone. Yet aloneness was never isolation. It was freedom.

Many wondered how he would survive after stepping away from the Theosophical world. The answer was simple. He needed little. He charged nothing for his talks. He asked for no gifts. He accumulated nothing. Books provided modest income. Friends helped when necessary. His life remained deliberately uncluttered.

The people who now gathered were different. They did not come seeking a Messiah. They came because they were restless, confused, wounded, or questioning. His voice was steady. His words were precise. There was no ritual, no promise. People often left feeling lighter. Not inspired in the usual sense, but unburdened.

He belonged nowhere. Yet he was at home everywhere. He moved from country to country, season to season. India. Europe. America and Latin America. He spoke in small halls and large tents, in schools, under trees, in city auditoriums. Even in his eighties he travelled tirelessly, speaking until only weeks before his death.

After the dissolution of the Order, Rajagopal offered to manage practical affairs once he completed his studies. He agreed easily. Administration did not interest him. Rajagopal organised schedules, publications, finances, and travel. For many years the arrangement worked smoothly.

But they were shaped by very different inner movements. He questioned everything, including himself. Rajagopal valued order and control. What began as small differences slowly hardened. Trust thinned. Disagreements deepened. By 1968, the separation had become unavoidable.

With that break, the earlier publishing system ended. Independent Krishnamurti Foundations arose in different countries. They carried no doctrine and no spiritual rank. Their purpose was practical, to preserve his talks accurately and support the schools that had grown around his work.

Ommen, once filled with bonfires and expectation, no longer called him back. The last camp there had been in 1938. Soon after, war broke out. The gatherings stopped.

The tents disappeared. Silence settled where voices had once risen in hope.

Then something darker came. The same quiet land was taken over and turned into a prison camp. People were brought there, held, and made to suffer. The fields that had once held stillness and trust now carried fear and pain. The air itself seemed changed. What had once been open and gentle could no longer remain untouched.

The peace that had filled Ommen did not return. He never went back.

After the separation from Rajagopal, Mary Zimbalist entered his life. Born Mary Taylor, she first heard Krishnamurti speak at Oak Grove in Ojai in 1944. The daughter of a prominent New York business family, she had worked as a fashion model and actress. At the time, she was deeply unhappy. Her meeting with Krishnamurti left a lasting impression on her.

She later married Sam Zimbalist, a well-known film producer. After her husband's death in 1958, Mary gradually returned to Krishnamurti's circle. In later years she chose to travel with him constantly, quietly managing many practical details of his life and serving as his devoted secretary.

His life had no anchors. No institution to shelter him. No ideology to steady him. No inner story to repeat.

One by one, the supports fell away.

What remained was astonishingly light. A human being moving without psychological weight.

He offered no system, no method, no directions. Only a call to look within oneself.

Seeing Clearly

By now he was speaking to thousands across the world. Those who heard him felt that he spoke from a depth of understanding that did not come from books or belief.

Yet the real question he asked was not about himself, but about how each person sees and understands life.

People came to hear him in many countries. Some expected spiritual guidance. Others hoped he would give them a new philosophy or method to follow.

Those who listened carefully, including teachers, scientists, and psychologists, noticed something unusual.

He did not speak from occult theories or philosophical ideas. Nor did he talk about God, mysticism, becoming enlightened, or leading a pious life. He was not explaining beliefs or repeating traditions. He was describing what he was seeing as it happened. His words did not feel constructed. They felt immediate.

Some leading psychologists admitted privately that he seemed to understand the human mind with unusual sharpness. Yet he did not analyse the mind piece by piece. He did not dissect it. He said the mind could only be understood in one sweep, in a single act of seeing.

He questioned one of psychology's most accepted methods: analysis. When you analyse yourself, he asked, who is the analyser? It is still thought. Still memory. Still the past judging itself. And the past cannot free itself from the past. What is conditioned cannot untangle conditioning.

Understanding comes in a different way. It comes when the mind sees without choosing. Without correcting. Without trying to become something else. In that instant of clear perception, the thing seen changes.

He also challenged the idea that the mind is divided into layers such as conscious and unconscious. To him, consciousness was one movement. When you see jealousy or fear clearly, you are not seeing a fragment. You are seeing the whole structure of yourself reflected in that moment.

It was not only what he said. It was how he lived. By the 1930s, he had grown into a striking presence. Not tall. Not imposing. Yet there was a natural dignity in the way he stood and walked. His movements were relaxed and precise. His eyes were bright and attentive. When he listened, he listened completely.

He dressed simply but with great care. Nothing about him was careless or excessive. His clothes were always neatly tailored and well kept. When travelling abroad he usually wore Western clothes, and Indian dress in India, blending easily with the people around him. He polished his own shoes until they shone and paid attention to even to the smallest details. The car he travelled in was kept clean and well cared for. His manners were gentle, his movements graceful, and his appearance quietly striking. There was a natural elegance about him that people noticed at once. Care and attention were present in everything he did.

In Indian villages, people sometimes folded their hands when he passed. They did not know his name. But they felt something quiet and steady in him.

George Bernard Shaw once remarked that Krishnamurti was the most beautiful person he had seen. Robinson Jeffers spoke not of beauty, but of presence. His wife said that when Krishnamurti entered a room, it was as if light entered with him. Yet he rejected every image made about him.

As the years passed, his language evolved. The core did not. Words shifted because language is limited. Seeing is not. He kept searching for simpler ways to speak about something that cannot be contained in speech.

When he spoke about meditation, he stripped the word of tradition. Meditation was not repetition. Not discipline. Not control. Not sitting rigidly with closed eyes. Meditation, he said, is the mind watching itself without interference. A stillness that comes naturally when there is understanding, not suppression.

He refused the role of guru. If someone bowed, he often bowed in return or stepped aside. Dependence, he said, weakens the mind. To rely on another for inner clarity is to postpone seeing for yourself.

He invited people to observe. Not analyse. Not judge. Just observe. Watch anger as it arises. Watch fear. Watch pleasure. The moment you say, "I must change this," conflict begins. But if you simply look, without naming, there is a different quality of attention.

Many found this difficult. The instant they tried to be aware, effort entered. He would say gently, notice that effort. That noticing is already awareness.

One of his most radical statements was that the observer is the observed.

You are not separate from your fear. You are not standing outside it. You are that movement. When this is seen directly, not thought about but actually seen, the division ends. And where division ends, conflict ends.

Education was close to his heart. He believed the world would change only when human beings learned to see clearly from childhood. Knowledge mattered.

But intelligence mattered more. Intelligence was not memory. It was the capacity to observe without fear.

He disliked comparison in schools. Competition, he felt, breeds anxiety and imitation. Children were not meant to become copies of each other. They were meant to understand themselves.

He founded schools where teachers were asked first to watch their own reactions. This was uncomfortable. To look at oneself without defence is never easy. When teachers hesitated, he would smile and say, "Just look. Do not try to become anything."

He warned against searching for truth in books alone. Books can inform. They cannot awaken. Truth is not hidden in distant places. It is hidden by inattention.

He enjoyed novels, poetry, humour, and films. He laughed easily. He was not solemn. Not distant. Not otherworldly.

He did not claim to be divine. He did not present himself as special. He was simply a human being who was free to see. And he suggested quietly and firmly that this freedom is not rare. It is there whenever you truly look.

Teacher Who Refused the Crown

Wherever he travelled, the same questions followed him. Was he the World Teacher? What was his message? And why did he refuse followers?

He did not answer in the way people expected. In his early talks, he spoke of freedom. Not the freedom to satisfy desire, but freedom from fear, from ambition, and from the constant pressure of becoming something. He questioned the heavy centre we call 'me', and asked whether that centre was the source of our conflict.

Life, he said, in its fullness is already here. Nothing new needs to be added. Nothing needs to be achieved. The mind is not empty because it lacks something; it is burdened because it carries too much, memory, comparison, fear, and hope. We are always trying to become something better, nobler, more secure. But in that effort, we miss what is right in front of us.

Most people are afraid of being nobody. They believe effort makes them worthy and struggle makes them strong. He challenged this deeply rooted idea. Virtue, he said, does not grow through struggle. When the mind is no longer trying to become, when it is simply attentive, there is a different quality of living. In that alertness, goodness appears naturally, without effort or reward.

He was equally clear that what he spoke was not meant for a spiritual elite. When asked whether his teaching was only for the chosen few, he replied that he had no interest in the chosen few. Either what is true is true for all human beings, or it has no meaning at all.

By the mid 1930s, rumours spread widely that he was the long awaited Teacher. At camps and gatherings he spoke with increasing intensity, not to build a new belief, but to dismantle illusion. He urged people to drop their inner crutches—beliefs that promised comfort, ideals that promised safety, authorities that promised guidance. These, he felt, weakened the mind instead of freeing it.

This disturbed many who loved him. Even Lady Emily felt shaken by what she heard. Confused and hurt, she wrote to him, asking whether he had denied being the World Teacher. In his reply, written privately to her, he was gentle but clear. He had never said he was not the one. But he added that it did not matter what he was called. Titles were distractions. The real question was simple. Is what is being said true? He explained that he was not opposing one organisation alone, but illusion wherever it existed. He could not remain silent, not out of pride, but because he saw clearly.

Those who knew him closely noticed something unusual. He could speak to monks, scientists, artists, and prime ministers without altering his tone. He did not argue or attempt to persuade. When something is seen clearly, explanation becomes simple. Mary Lutyens later wrote that while others debated endlessly, Krishnamurti seemed to hold truth directly, as if in the palm of his hand.

That clarity showed itself even in difficult situations. In 1950 he addressed a hall of noisy, mocking students in Colombo. They laughed and interrupted him. He did not scold them or withdraw. He listened. When they demanded to know whether he was the Christ, he did not defend himself. Instead, he spoke about his own childhood, his loneliness, his confusion, and his search. Gradually the noise softened. Curiosity replaced ridicule. By the end, many who had come to mock were listening quietly.

Again and again, people who could not fully explain him said something honest. They did not know why, but something in what he said felt true.

Many spiritual teachers lived in his time, figures such as Sri Aurobindo and Ramana Maharshi, each with depth and devoted followers. He stood apart, not as higher or lower, but as direct. He offered no ritual, no ceremony, no priesthood, and no system to practise. He did not ask anyone to believe or to follow.

The writer Henry Miller once tried to describe what made him unique. What struck Miller most was his complete inward openness, his "nakedness." If he had a mission, Miller suggested, it was to strip away illusion, to knock down the false supports people leaned on, and to return to them the dignity of standing alone. Even though he had once been proclaimed the World Teacher, Miller felt that what mattered was not the title itself, but the rare quality of a mind that refused authority.

He never asked the world to crown him. He refused every title that was placed upon him. What mattered was not who he was, but whether one could see clearly for oneself.

He did not promise salvation. He did not offer comfort.

He asked for honesty. He pointed toward awareness.

The Empty Vessel

For more than sixty years, he travelled across the world, city after city, country after country. He did not retire into silence to write doctrines. He did not try to build a system of ideas. He did not set out to create a philosophy, nor did he think of himself as a philosopher. He spoke. He met people face to face. He listened to their questions and responded freshly each time. Almost everything we know about his teaching comes from these living conversations, later written down and shared with others.

He spoke about fear, sorrow, love, death, and freedom. The subjects appeared different, yet there was no division in what he said. It was one movement, like water taking many shapes, yet remaining water. Again and again, he reminded listeners not to accept his words. Truth, he insisted, cannot be handed over. It must be seen directly.

Many wondered how such clarity had come into being. Was there a sudden awakening? Had it been the result of long discipline?

He dismissed such ideas. Nothing extraordinary had 'happened' to him, he said. There had been no spiritual explosion. What was there had always been there. It unfolded naturally, without ambition or design.

Those near him noticed the care with which he treated the body. He exercised daily, walked long distances, ate lightly, and rested when needed. He lived as though the body had been entrusted to him, not owned by him. Once he remarked that, had it not been worn down by constant travel, it might have lasted a few hundred years.

Outwardly, he was refined but unassuming. Not tall, yet upright. His movements were precise and relaxed. When he entered a room, the atmosphere often shifted quietly. What people sensed was not physical beauty alone. It was order, simplicity, and an absence of strain.

The deeper beauty was inward.

Even as a child, there was something unusual about him. His mind did not seem to hold what it received. He later said that he had been like a vessel with holes in it; whatever was poured into it simply passed through, leaving nothing behind. To those around him, this often appeared as vagueness or dullness. He struggled at school, could not remember his lessons, and was sometimes punished for it. Later, he explained that the mind was simply not grasping or possessing what it encountered. It was open, yet it did not hold.

Those who observed him closely spoke of a mind empty of self. Not vacant, not indifferent, but free from the constant noise of becoming, the restless movement of always trying to be something more or different. It was a mind that did not carry things from one moment to the next, did not cling, did not resist experience. It saw, and in seeing, the experience ended.

Such a mind was not dull. It was deeply alive, fresh, and attentive, like a clear sky after rain.

In rare moments of openness, he acknowledged something even more radical. There was no inner centre that said "I." The body functioned. Memory functioned when needed. But the psychological centre most people defend so fiercely was absent. There was awareness, but no one who owned it.

In later years, in very private conversations, he spoke of something that surprised many. He said that what had once been described as the consciousness of Lord Maitreya had wholly merged in him. The personal centre called Krishnamurti no longer remained as an ego. He did not elaborate, nor did he present this publicly. Those who heard him understood that he was not reviving an old belief or inviting worship. He spoke of it simply as a fact of his inner life, without emphasis or interpretation.

He never allowed such statements to become doctrine. For him, names and forms were secondary. What mattered was whether the mind was free of self.

To many, the word 'empty' sounds cold or lifeless. But the emptiness he spoke of was not absence. It was freedom from accumulation. Like a clear mirror that reflects everything yet holds nothing, the mind was free because it did not carry yesterday into today. Each meeting was new. Each question fresh.

He spoke of death in the same way. To let an experience end completely, without holding on to it, was to live without burden. Ending inwardly was not loss; it was renewal.

It meant not carrying yesterday into today. When the mind does not cling, there is no fear of ending. Then death is not something waiting at the end of life. It becomes a part of living.

Those who sat quietly with him sometimes noticed that conversation would suddenly stop. He would fall into complete stillness. It was not deliberate. It was not a technique. It was simply that thought had come to rest. In that silence, nothing dramatic happened, yet something was deeply alive. One felt no pressure to become anything. There was only attention.

There was also a quiet kindness in that stillness, something gentle that made others feel at ease without a word being spoken.

He refused to let any of this become mystical. He warned against turning inner freedom into a goal. The moment one seeks to imitate such a state, effort begins, and effort belongs to the self. The self cannot dissolve itself through will. It ends when it is seen clearly.

He offered no comfort through promise. Instead, he invited something far more demanding, to observe your life without escape. Watch fear as it moves. Watch desire as it forms. Watch hurt as it arises. Not to change it, not to improve it, but simply to see.

At first this feels stark. There is no structure to lean on, no authority to reassure. But in direct observation there is a different kind of security, not born of belief but of clarity. When there is clear seeing, intelligence operates effortlessly.

His teaching contained no formulas, no sacred techniques, no spiritual ladders. He did not tell people what to practise. He pointed only to attention, attention without motive, without direction, without conclusion.

And in the presence of such attention, something both extraordinary and utterly natural seemed to happen.

The Healing Hand

There were also times when those who lived close to him felt something unusual. While he spoke against claims of power and discouraged such ideas, small things seemed to shift quietly in his presence. Houses troubled by tension felt calmer. Plants that had been neglected slowly came back to life. Rain would arrive after long spells of dryness. Those who noticed such things spoke of them quietly among themselves.

Something about him seemed to affect the atmosphere around him.

He brushed all this aside. He did not want to be surrounded by stories.

From childhood, he was aware of a certain healing quality in his hands. People in pain would sit before him. He would touch them lightly or move his hands slowly in the air over them. Many said they felt relief. Some claimed recovery from serious illness.

He did not speak much about such things or organise healing sessions. He kept away from drawing attention to them and discouraged interest in what might appear extraordinary.

One of the early accounts concerned a young man named Dwarak, born with a severe heart condition. He could hardly walk, and treatment in those days was limited. When he was brought to him, he was seen daily. He would place his hand gently upon Dwarak's chest and make slow, sweeping movements. At first the pain intensified, then gradually subsided. Years later, Dwarak said he had been completely cured and believed he owed his life to him.

Illness also touched his own extended family. Padmanabham, the son of Sivaram's eldest daughter, underwent surgery at the Christian Medical College Hospital in Vellore. Doctors gave little hope of survival. When he was brought to him, he too received healing passes. His condition improved. He studied at Bangalore University and lived a few more years than expected.

One year, however, he was unable to return to India. Padmanabham's health deteriorated rapidly, and he died at the age of twenty-two. Later, when Narayan met him in England, he approached him quietly and said, "I am sorry for the boy. I could not come this year." He seemed already to know.

In another case, a man suffering from an advanced eye disease had been told that nothing further could be done.

His sight was fading rapidly. For nearly a month, he gently touched the man's eyes and made slow passes with his hands. Gradually the man's vision improved. The hair he had touched appeared darker again, though the rest remained grey.

Some who lived near him noticed another curious effect. Jayalakshmi, who hosted him during his visits to Madras, recalled that he would sometimes hold her bangles quietly in his hands for a few minutes before returning them. She felt they had become strangely magnetised by his touch and believed they carried a healing influence within them. An old friend, Jamnadas Dwarkadas, remembered similar occasions when he would hold his rings for a while and return them. Whether this was imagination or something more subtle, those around him felt that his touch seemed to carry a quiet vitality.

Perhaps the most striking account was one he himself narrated to Narayan. A woman had severely injured her knee. The joint had not healed; infection had set in, and doctors had recommended amputation. She was carried on a stretcher to meet him.

He stepped out onto the verandah and their eyes met.

For a moment, nothing happened.

Then slowly she began to move. She rose, unassisted. Within moments she was standing. Then walking. Her husband stood speechless.

When Narayan later asked how such a thing could happen, he replied simply, "Somewhere, something clicks."

"What clicks?" Narayan asked.

"Energy passes."

He said nothing further.

When pressed about these matters, he would say only that the healing quality had been there from early years. He asked Narayan not to speak publicly of such things. If word spread, he said, there would be endless queues seeking cures.

He himself once explained why he never encouraged healing. Speaking in London in 1931, he said that he had once healed a friend, only to see the same man later imprisoned for a crime. Physical cures, he said, do not necessarily change the mind or heart. "Which would you rather have," he asked, "a teacher who momentarily heals your wounds, or one who shows you the way to remain whole?"

He did not wish to become known as a healer. Physical relief, he felt, was secondary. The real suffering of human beings lay deeper, in fear, confusion, sorrow, and the endless search for security. To cure the body without addressing the mind was incomplete.

He would often ask, "Does this free the human being?" If something did not bring clarity, he felt it was not essential.

He refused to gather people through wonder or miracles.

Whatever took place around him, he allowed it to remain simple, without explanation, without claim, without conclusion.

Those Who Walked With Him

Krishnamurti has often been described as the seer who walked alone.

Yet no one truly walks through life alone.

The words capture something essential about him. He refused to belong to any religious tradition. He rejected spiritual authority and would not allow anyone to follow him as a guru.

Yet the picture of a solitary figure tells only part of the story.

For although he walked alone in spirit, many quietly walked beside him in life. Their names rarely appear in the foreground, but without them the story of his life would feel incomplete.

He himself wrote very little. Most of the books that carry his name grew out of his talks and dialogues with people around the world. Only a few were written directly by him, such as *Krishnamurti's Notebook*, *Krishnamurti's Journal*, and *Krishnamurti to Himself.* Earlier works such as *The First and Last Freedom* and the three volumes of *Commentaries on Living* were also shaped from his conversations and reflections.

The fuller story of his life has been preserved through remarkable biographies by those who knew him personally. Among the most important are the works of Mary Lutyens and Pupul Jayakar.

In earlier times, great spiritual teachers gathered disciples around them—forming a *sangha* or orders of monks. He would have none of that. Again and again he insisted there were no followers and no spiritual hierarchy around him.

Yet many lives were deeply touched by him. Those who came close did not receive titles or positions. Instead they received something far more valuable. They were challenged to look directly at themselves and discover truth for themselves.

While there were no disciples in the traditional sense, there were many who walked with him and helped carry forward the spirit of inquiry he awakened.

Among his closest companions in India was Pupul Jayakar.

Pupul Jayakar became one of his close companions during the later years of his life. A gifted writer and cultural historian, she organised many of his talks and dialogues in India. Her home often became a meeting place where long conversations unfolded late into the evening. He would question those around him with great intensity, asking them to look deeply into the nature of thought, fear, and freedom.

Through her biography, she preserved an intimate and vivid record of the teacher and his extraordinary life.

Pupul's sisters Nandini Mehta and Premlata Mehta were also part of this close circle. In his later life, when the intense physical episodes known as the Process happened, Pupul Jayakar and Nandini Mehta cared for him.

The Process rarely happened in the presence of anyone who was not deeply trusted by him.

With time a younger generation also entered this circle. Pupul Jayakar's daughter, Radhika Herzberger, Nandini Mehta's daughter, Devyani, and Asit Chandmal, the son of her sister Premlata, grew up knowing him from an early age. They saw him not as a distant spiritual figure but as someone who moved naturally in their lives.

Radhika Herzberger later became a distinguished scholar and educator. For many years she worked closely with the schools inspired by his vision of education and served as Director of the Rishi Valley Education Centre. Her work helped nurture an environment where learning was not merely about examinations but about awakening intelligence, sensitivity, and understanding.

There were many others who shared in discussions with him.

In Bombay, a circle of friends often gathered for conversations. Among them were Achyut Patwardhan, a freedom fighter who later turned toward philosophy, his brother Pama Patwardhan and his wife Sunanda. In a later generation, Rajesh Dalal, an engineer trained at IIT, chose to work in the schools instead of pursuing a conventional career. For a time, he also served as Director of the Rajghat Education Centre.

Some people worked closely with him in the schools that grew around his educational vision. Professor P. Krishna became deeply involved in this work and later shared his personal experiences with many students and teachers. Balasundaram, who had been Director of the Besant School at Rajghat, was also unusually close to him.

Friends such as Mark Lee and his wife Asha Lee were deeply connected with the educational communities around the schools. Mark Lee had earlier taught at Rishi Valley School, where he met Asha, whom he later married. He later became the founding director of the Oak Grove School in Ojai. Both were close to him.

Writers and poets also found their way to him. Among them were the novelist Aldous Huxley and the poet Robinson Jeffers.

His friendships extended far beyond philosophers, writers, and poets to include internationally respected scientists.

The physicist David Bohm, often described as a titan of theoretical physics, entered into many deep dialogues with him over the years. Other scientists, including E. C. G. Sudarshan, also joined these discussions.

The German industrialist Friedrich Grohe, who later lived in Switzerland, supported his work for many years and played a significant role in preserving the teachings.

Among those who cared for him closely was Dr Pachure, his trusted physician in India.

He had long before severed all organisational ties with the Theosophical Society. In his later years, he nevertheless maintained a warm personal friendship with Radha Burnier, who served for many years as President of the Society at Adyar. She had known him from her childhood. When they met, their conversations were quiet and affectionate, and she listened with deep attention.

After his death, many friends wrote memoirs of their encounters with him. These recollections help us glimpse the teacher not only on the platform but in the quiet moments of daily life.

The story told in this book has followed him mainly through the years of his childhood and early awakening. Yet his life continued to unfold for many decades after that.

If those later years been described in full, the many individuals who walked beside him would appear again and again in the narrative. They listened, questioned, organised meetings, taught in the schools, and helped preserve the spirit of inquiry he awakened.

To understand why this quiet man from India touched so many lives, we must now look more closely at the teacher himself.

He may indeed have walked alone.

Yet around him moved a quiet constellation of men and women, each touched by the light he pointed to. Their names may not stand at the centre of the story, yet without them the story would lose the quiet human warmth that surrounded the man who spoke of freedom.

But the most remarkable thing about Krishnamurti was not the number of people who walked beside him, nor the respect he received from thinkers, writers, and leaders around the world. What made him truly extraordinary was the way he spoke and the way he pointed people back to themselves.

He asked no one to follow him, yet millions listened.

He offered no system, yet his words awakened deep questions in countless minds.

He gave no answers, yet something in his words remained. It stayed with people, quietly working long after they had gone.

A Teacher Like No Other

Through the centuries, humanity has known many great teachers. Some founded religions. Some performed miracles. Some wrote sacred books that shaped civilisations. Their words gathered followers, and their names became institutions.

Krishnamurti did none of these things.

He did not begin a new religion. He did not accept worship. He did not claim to be a prophet, a saviour, or a divine messenger. Instead, he questioned the very instinct to follow. He stood without titles, without hierarchy, and without spiritual ornament. In doing so, he stood alone.

What made him different was not that he rejected tradition, but that he refused dependence. He would not allow his teaching to be turned into a system. It had to remain alive, like air that belongs to everyone and cannot be bottled.

He did not stand above people. He stood beside them. He did not offer comfort through belief or promise reward through faith. He asked something much simpler and far more demanding. Look at your life directly. Look at fear, loneliness, ambition, and sorrow, without escape and without explanation.

He also refused comparison. People tried to measure him against the Buddha, against Jesus, and against other spiritual figures. But comparison, he said, is measurement, and truth cannot be measured. The moment we compare, we move away from understanding and fall into admiration or criticism.

Many spiritual traditions speak of gradual improvement, discipline, control, practice, and purification. Step by step, they say, the human being becomes better. Effort refines the mind. Time perfects the soul.

Krishnamurti approached it differently. He was not teaching people what to think, but helping them learn to see.

Instead of asking how to improve the self, he asked what the self actually is. What is this centre that struggles, compares, fears, desires, and seeks continuity? Is it something permanent, or only a movement of memory and thought?

That question was radical. He was not interested in decorating the cage. He asked whether the cage exists at all when it is observed completely.

For him, freedom was not the final reward of practice. It was the ending of confusion now, in the very act of seeing clearly. When there is clear perception, there is no gradual path. There is understanding.

Many people find Krishnamurti difficult for this reason. They try to understand him through thought, through old knowledge, and through words alone. But thought itself is often the barrier. The more we analyse, the farther we move from simple perception.

In his talks, listeners sometimes felt that he never gave clear conclusions. They expected formulas, paths, and instructions about what to do or not to do, as many teachers of the past had given. But Krishnamurti did not offer ready answers or final results. Instead, he tried to show something directly, like pointing to a view from a hill.

And a view cannot be explained step by step. It can only be seen with one's own eyes.

Because people were used to explanations and conclusions, they often felt his teaching was difficult, when in fact it asked only that they look for themselves. His words cannot truly be explained by anyone else. They have to be heard or read directly, with a quiet mind. Only then can the words touch the mind deeply and begin to flower.

This may sound difficult at first. But Krishnamurti was not asking young people to become scholars or saints. He was asking them to notice simple things, a moment of jealousy, a hurt feeling, the wish to be praised, the fear of being left out. In such small moments, he felt, the whole movement of the mind could be seen.

That was why his words touched some people so deeply. He was not speaking about distant spiritual matters. He was speaking about the hidden struggles of everyday life, the loneliness no one sees, the comparisons that quietly wound us, the fears we cover up with smiles. To listen to him seriously was to feel someone was asking us, perhaps for the first time, to be completely honest.

He never constructed grand explanations or built philosophical systems. He invited direct perception. He often insisted, "Do not believe me. Let us look together." But looking together requires stillness, and stillness is rare.

He was often described as a great thinker or philosopher. But he was neither. A philosopher builds ideas and systems through thought. Krishnamurti was not doing that. He was pointing to something that becomes visible when thought becomes quiet. His words were not meant to create a philosophy. They were meant to awaken intelligence, an intelligence of a different kind.

When one truly listened, without resistance, without comparison, and without trying to become, something unexpected sometimes happened. There was a sudden clarity. Not the result of effort or analysis, but a direct perception that did not depend on thought.

He never gave this a sacred name. He never claimed it as an achievement. Yet many sensed that something in his words quietly awakened intelligence.

This was not the intelligence we usually mean by intelligence. What we often call intelligence is intellect. We study, think, compare, and practise until knowledge grows. Intellect helps us understand things and form ideas from what we know. But it has its limits.

He, by contrast, seemed to be pointing to something entirely different. In listening to him, one had the sense that intelligence was not merely the slow growth of knowledge through effort, practice, or accumulation. It appeared in moments of clear seeing. When the mind looked without fear, without choosing, and without trying to become something, perception seemed to become direct and immediate.

This kind of seeing, an intelligence of a different order, does not depend on time, authority, or spiritual stages. Nor is it an attainment. It is a silent flowering.

He used reasoning only to point beyond reasoning. What he invited people to discover was something much simpler, the freedom of seeing clearly for oneself. Intelligence awakens the moment the mind sees without illusion, and in that instant the whole movement of confusion can end.

In that way he became a teacher who quietly redefined what spirituality truly means.

When asked in Rajghat, "Sir, do you deny the Masters?" he replied calmly, "No, I have never denied the Masters. But what was sublime was made ridiculous, and I denied the ridiculous."

He did not dismiss unusual experiences or hidden powers. In later life, when asked about initiations, he spoke to Balasundaram, one of his close associates, and made something very clear. "Those things exist," he said.

"It is another form of power. It has nothing to do with goodness, so I am not interested in it."

For him, power and goodness belonged to completely different worlds.

Though he moved away from Theosophy, he spoke of it without bitterness. In later years he remarked, "I think they touched something real, but then tried to make it concrete, to put it into symbols, and so lost it." Truth, he seemed to suggest, fades when we try to organise it.

He spoke with deep respect of the Buddha. When asked which teacher came closest to the truths of life, he answered, "The Buddha... the Buddha comes closer than any other. Though I am not myself a Buddhist."

Yet even here he would not allow reverence to become belief. Once he said, "Perhaps the Buddha saw that intelligence has nothing to do with thought. Others turned that into methods." In a moment of warmth he added, "If the Buddha talked to me, I would say, 'Sir, I listen because I love you, not because I want to become something.'"

Then he said something startling. "Nobody listened to him, that is why there is Buddhism."

He did not mean disrespect. Rather, he meant that when insight becomes structure, fresh listening ends.

Many asked him, "What is truth?" During a discussion in England, a respected scholar pressed him, "Please tell me now, what is truth?" Krishnamurti replied quietly, "You want to know truth in one minute, sir? It is compassion, and there is no illusion in it."

He was very clear that after his death no one was to claim authority over his teaching. "The speaker has no authority," he would say. "If you follow him, you destroy yourself." The moment someone interprets, thought interferes. Opinion enters. What was clear becomes second-hand.

He once said that the teaching itself was sacred, not the teacher. The person did not matter. What mattered was the living truth being pointed to.

During the final weeks of his life in Ojai in 1986, he asked a quiet question. "How is the perfume to be carried on?" Then he added gently, "My wish is that the perfume should be carried on."

For many years he had also warned that the teaching must never be interpreted or turned into authority. "From the nineteen twenties," he once said, "I have been saying that there should be no interpreters of the teachings." If someone claimed to explain it for others, he felt that the living truth could easily become distorted.

For this reason, while he was still alive, a few foundations were created simply to preserve the original talks, writings, and recordings exactly as they were. These include the Krishnamurti Foundation India, the Krishnamurti Foundation America, the Krishnamurti Foundation Trust in England, and the Fundación Krishnamurti Latinoamericana, which serves the Spanish-speaking world.

Their responsibility is not to interpret the teaching, but to protect the original words and make them available to everyone.

Today, in the age of digital media and artificial intelligence, recordings sometimes appear that sound like Krishnamurti but are not genuine. For a careful reader or listener, it therefore becomes important to return to the original talks, books, and recordings preserved by these foundations.

Krishnamurti had always insisted that each person must look and discover for oneself. But he also wished that the perfume of the teaching should not be altered.

He did not deny the body, nor did he glorify it. The body eats, sleeps, ages, and dies. It has its own intelligence. But it is not the centre of identity. When the mind no longer builds its image around the body, life takes its natural place.

Perhaps that is why he remains difficult to place among other teachers. He founded nothing, demanded nothing, promised nothing.

It was freedom from the self, a revolution that begins within and remains within, perhaps the only true revolution.

He invited them to discover freedom.

And freedom cannot be named or crowned.

Adieu

Some people move through life as if time stretches endlessly before them.

Krishnamurti, whom many simply called K, sometimes spoke as though he sensed the road would end sooner than others imagined.

In 1985, while in England, he quietly told a few close friends that he had an inward feeling about his death. He did not wish to discuss details. To fix dates or speculate, he felt, would be the mind interfering, an attempt by the ego to control even the last moment. His life, he said, had its own movement. When it ended, that ending would be clear.

In the final days, he spoke more openly of something he had rarely touched upon. For many years, he said, an immense energy and intelligence had worked through the body, a body that had been carefully prepared and sustained. After so many years, the body could no longer bear it. When it ended, it ended completely. What had taken place could not be repeated or imitated.

By late 1985, his health declined sharply. A respected doctor in Madras suspected something serious. Tests were advised. At first he hesitated, not out of fear, but because he did not want hospitals and anxiety to interrupt the few remaining talks he felt responsible to give.

His last public talk took place on 4 January 1986 at Vasanta Vihar in Madras. He spoke of religion, the brain and the mind, the impact of computers, creativity, and the mystery of existence. He asked whether the brain could ever be clear, free of tradition, conditioning, and constant noise. He urged listeners not to wait for guidance. If life is confused, it must change now.

Then he turned to the question of ending. Why wait until the body fails? he asked. Is it possible to die each day to memory, to hurt, to attachment? When yesterday ends, today is fresh. When there is no clinging, there is strength.

At the close, he stopped. After a long silence, he asked if they would sit quietly together for a few minutes. It was not a farewell. It was shared stillness.

On 10 January, he left India for the final time and travelled to Ojai, California. The journey was painful. Examinations revealed advanced cancer. Even then, his attention remained alert. He showed little interest in sympathy. What mattered to him was clarity.

He had always treated the body carefully, simply, attentively. Even when he required a blood transfusion, he asked that the donor live cleanly.

As weakness increased, he asked to leave the hospital and return to Pine Cottage. He did not want machines around him at the end. Nurses attended quietly. Medication was given, but he made one request very clear. The mind must remain clear. Excess pain, he said, clouded something subtle, what he sometimes referred to as 'the other'.

About ten days before his death, he spoke with unusual firmness. For nearly seventy years, he said, an immense energy and intelligence had worked through the body. Few understood what it meant. The body had been prepared and protected for decades. Without such care, he felt, it could not have sustained that intensity.

He was equally clear about something else. When the body ends, that state ends. It does not continue as a personal presence. It cannot be contacted. It does not hover somewhere, waiting.

"When he goes, it goes," he said quietly. He warned against creating stories or seeking connection after death. Imagination easily becomes illusion. What mattered was not reaching him, but living what had been pointed to.

In his final days, the body grew frail, but the mind remained lucid. He spoke quietly about practical matters. He wanted no rituals, no worship, no gathering around the body. It had done its work.

On the evening of Sunday, 16 February 1986, the pain eased. Around seven o'clock, he took a sleeping pill and gently asked those near him to go to bed. He repeated this with concern for their rest. He fell asleep. The sleep deepened into a coma. His breathing grew softer, slower.

In the early hours of 17 February 1986, at ten minutes past midnight, his heart came to rest.

There was no proclamation. Only stillness.

In the morning, the body was washed and wrapped simply in khadi silk. Those present noticed a softness in the face. No crowd gathered. The cremation was quiet.

His ashes were later divided, as he had wished. Some remained in America. Some were taken to England. In India, portions were immersed at places that marked his life, Rajghat, the source of the Ganga in the Himalayas, the shore at Adyar where his public journey began, and Rishi Valley, where a small part was buried on a hill he loved.

Nothing was announced. Nothing was claimed. The world quietly said adieu.

Perhaps the best way to remember him is not through statues or repetition. He asked only that you look at your thoughts, your fears, your pleasures, just as they are, without condemning or escaping.

If even once you see clearly, without distortion or motive, something remarkable happens. The intelligence he spoke of is no longer something that belongs to a teacher. It is there.

This book does not end in sorrow but in quietness. When a teacher leaves you free, there is no one to follow, only the responsibility of seeing for yourself. And if, in some silent moment, you look at the world freshly, without fear or memory, then the empty vessel has done its work.

9 789358 121292

Printed at Repro India Ltd.